Cherita Houston is the founder of Independent Living After The Storm Transitional Living Program, a nonprofit organization for women and children. What began as a passion and a fire burning from within has turned into a reality. She lives and continues to serve in Chicago with her four boys.

This book is dedicated to every woman who has ever found herself going through a silent storm but kept pushing, persevering, and smiling through it all, knowing that her outcome would be greater than she could ever imagine, ask, or think.

Cherita Houston

THE ALPHA WOMAN IN CHRIST

AUSTIN MACAULEY PUBLISHERS™

LONDON * CAMBRIDGE * NEW YORK * SHARJAH

Ordering Information
Quantity sales: Special discounts are available on quantity purchases by corporations, associations, and others. For details, contact the publisher at the address below.

Publisher's Cataloging-in-Publication data
Houston, Cherita
The Alpha Woman in Christ

ISBN 9781643781495 (Paperback)
ISBN 9781643781501 (Hardback)
ISBN 9781647508845 (ePub e-book)

Library of Congress Control Number: 2021907842

www.austinmacauley.com/us

First Published (2021)
Austin Macauley Publishers LLC
40 Wall Street, 33rd Floor, Suite 3302
New York, NY 10005
USA

mail-usa@austinmacauley.com
+1 (646) 5125767

I would like to acknowledge first and foremost my Heavenly Father. Without Him I am nothing.

My four sons – Kenyon, Shannon, Landen, and Langston –who have taught me how to truly live selflessly and the true meaning of unconditional love.

My mother, who gave me the blueprint to what a strong woman is by the examples she sets forth through the way she lives.

My father, who, no matter what, provided for his family by any means necessary.

My brother, who has always shown me kindness, gentleness, and the definition of what a true man looks like.

My sister, who has persistently demonstrated to me how to be bold and unapologetic in what I feel and believe in.

My cousin, more like my sister, T.W., who's been in my life since I've known I had one. The truest of friends, never judging, always with a listening ear, open, and willing to help in any way possible.

My spiritual coach/mentor, Mrs. Madelyn, for seeing in me what I couldn't see in myself and her unceasing prayers.

Last but certainly not least, Mr. A.H., who has only been in my life a short amount of time but has made an impact like he's been here forever. He has shown me that I can have my fairy tale here on earth.

Chapter 1
The Alpha Woman

The alpha woman is a strong, royal female. She can often be intimidating to those around her and is not afraid to ask for what she wants. She is successful in her career and has a solid foundation to rely on. There is nothing quite as vivid as a woman with sureness and drive.

When most people hear the expression "female alpha," they automatically reflect on the most eye-catching, influential or dominant woman they know. Nevertheless, female alphas are not so easily identifiable. They might be beautiful or bossy or even authoritative, but this is not what defines them.

She is a woman completely in control, along with God, of her destiny. She is usually a loner, alpha women are home bodies and really flourish in their alone time, but does go to friends when she is ready. Alpha women cannot be categorized and will always rise above the stereotype of being just a "female."

I know oh-so-well about the alpha woman because I am her. In the past I have tried to calm it, but now I embrace it. I tried to dim the light on my alpha-ism because it was frowned upon and subjected to people that could not handle its value. So I was told things like I was too controlling and always wanted things my way but that was not the case at all; it was just the fact that I knew who I was, my purpose in life, and how I was and am to go about getting things accomplished. Because of some people's lack of knowledge or incapability of handling "The Alpha Woman," they often become offended by way of the things I say, but by no means is that ever my intention to offend anyone. This is just who I am and always have been. Being an Alpha is one of God's greatest gifts.

What is Alpha and Omega?

Alpha and Omega are the first and last letters of the Greek alphabet, hence, symbolically, "beginning and end"; in Revelation "The Eternal One" in (Rev. 1:8) of the Father, in (Rev. 2:16) and (Rev. 22:13) of the Son. Greek letters the first and the last, did the Lord put on Himself, symbols of the beginning and the end meeting in Him, in order that just as alpha rolls on to omega and omega returns again to alpha, so He might show that both the evolution of the beginning to the end is in Him and again the return of the end to the beginning.

Bible Reference

Esther 4:16 (A Courageous Queen) 'Go gather together all the Jews that are present in Shu'-shan, and fast yet for me, and neither eat nor drink three days, night or day: I also and my maidens will fast likewise; and so will I go in unto the king, which`` is not according to the law: and if I perish, I perish.

How could the modern-day woman imagine the fear and insecurity that would plague Queen Esther, who was chosen solely on the basis of her beauty and appeal to the king? She was no princess with the clout of her father's kingdom to enhance her position in the court. When she was not summoned for thirty days, she did not know if the king had found someone more pleasing or if she was merely losing her influence.

As a displaced, orphan Jewess, Esther had been reared by Mordecai, an older relative. Whether by his bidding, by force of evil officials, or by her own choice, she had entered the beauty contest and won. Now Mordecai's sources informed Esther that the Jewish people were scheduled for extinction by the wicked man Haman, a self-promoter who had elevated himself to vice-regent, second only to the monarch, King Ahasuerus.

Faced with a desperate challenge to survive, Esther pondered Mordecai's question: "Who knoweth whether thou art come to the kingdom for such a time as this?" (Esth. 4:14)

Three principles came to life in his advance:

- No place of privilege can ever exempt a person from responsibility to respond to God's call.
- Although a situation may look hopeless, God is never helpless.
- A God-given opportunity is an individual's received privilege.

Courageously, Esther formulated her plan, even if it meant dying in the effort. In the court she had been taught to prepare herself physically, but she had also learned to prepare herself spiritually, as was evident by her fasting (Esther 4:16; 9:31). With patience, the queen invited Ahasuerus and Haman to a pair of banquets. Then, seizing the right moment, she presented her case, not questioning the kin's justice or righteousness, but humbly asking for mercy for herself and her people.

Divine guidance seemingly directed Esther's thoughts, words, and actions. She had won the respect and the ear of her royal husband. In response, he assigned to her the task of re-writing the law (Esther 9:29), and she became quite properly the heroine of her people. To every woman she is a reminder of God's sovereignty. God used her beauty, her intelligence, and perhaps even her respectful attitude toward her husband, as well as remarkable, fearless faith to accomplish His will. Though her obedience, Esther became the true "star" in the Kingdom.

Esther carried the attributes of "The Alpha Woman."
Graciousness a Complement to Beauty

A gracious spirit enhances an alpha woman in Christ demeanor, while a selfish heart tarnishes her appearance and limits her effectiveness. The word "gracious" is used to describe God Himself (Ex. 34:6; Neh. 9:17; Ps. 111:4). Abigail was a gracious a woman. She realized and accepted her husband's weak habits (1 Sam. 25:23-31). She poised herself before David with respect, kindness, and courtesy. Yet in so doing, she showed deference to her husband and others by taking upon herself responsibility for the lack of hospitality.

The Moabite Ruth was a quiet woman whose perseverance complemented her beauty. She was gracious to her mother-in-law even when Naomi was absorbed in bitterness and self-pity (Ruth 2:2). Her strong character and gracious manner were eventually rewarded with a devoted husband and important offspring (Ruth 4:13). Having experienced God's forgiveness and love should increase an alpha woman in Christ's sensitivity to another's needs.

A condescending or resentful attitude does not exemplify graciousness. Alpha women in Christ are challenged to be gracious, kind, merciful, and forgiving (Neh. 9:17).

An alpha woman in Christ reflects God's kingdom by words spoken. Wise words are gracious, but foolish words are damaging (Eccl. 10:12). Alpha women in Christ are also admonished to speak with kindness and truth (Col. 3:12, 13). Words can scar the heart and forever damage a reputation and relationship. To possess graciousness is to showcase His love and channel His care to a needy world. As and in itself, graciousness or charm is merely a pleasing manner which has been developed through painstaking determination to do certain things in order to win the favor of family and friends. In other words, it is an outward polish or refinement. Furthermore, if this graciousness is the fruit of Godly character, springing from a heart committed to the Lord, then such charm becomes a tool for drawing other to the Savior and for service to Christ in the kingdom. Such a "gracious" woman retains a great honor.

He Is the Essence of Grace

Grace and mercy fraternal twins. They are initiated by the same person, springing from the same source, and appear simultaneously, but they are not identical. Mercy does not give us what we do deserve; grace gives us what we do not deserve. "Grace" denotes goodwill, kindness, and benefit. It evokes images of a superior granting favors to an undeserving inferior. The Lord's grace includes undeserved favor, unexpected acceptance, and unconditional love.

Jesus is the giver of grace (John 1:14, 17). A sample of "grace gifts" include: salvation (Eph. 2:8), adoption (Eph. 1:5), inheritance (Eph. 1:11), heavenly citizenship (Phil. 3:20), holiness (Eph. 1:4), access to God (Eph. 2:18), forgiveness (Eph. 1:7), preparation for service (1 Pet. 2:5-9), the indwelling of the Holy Spirit (Eph. 1:13), the armor of God (Eph. 6:10-18), and much more. No wonder His grace is called "manifold" (1 Pet. 4:10). Sin is not match for God's grace. Whatever sin's impact may be, His grace is more potent (Rom. 5:20). God is a giving God. He gives out of His love and loves to give. Grace is one of His greatest pleasures (Eph. 1:5, 9).

Salvation: God's Deliverance

Salvation can be described as "snatching" someone from serious danger. Just as you would "snatch" your child from before an oncoming automobile to save his life, the Lord Jesus saves or "snatches" every alpha woman in Christ who trusts in Him from the pathway that leads to eternal death in Hell (Rom. 6:23). Salvation can best be understood as God's deliverance. In the Old Testament, God delivered Israel from their enemies many times (Judg. 3:9, 15, 28). In the New Testament, God delivered sinners from eternity in Hell (Acts 16:31).

Salvation requires not only God's initial action but also your response. There are basically three aspects of God's salvation or deliverance: justification, sanctification, and glorification. Justification is God's deliverance from sin's penalty. When a woman accepts Christ into her life, she becomes totally free from the penalty of sin and spiritual death (Rom. 3:23-25). The penalty for sins that have been committed in the past or sins that will be committed in the future has been paid through the death of Jesus Christ on the Cross.

Sanctifications is God's progressive deliverance of an alpha woman in Christ from sin's power (Eph. 5:26; 1 Thess. 5:23). God's desire is that a believer mature and become more Christ-like, that she become free from sin's control in her life. But if the alpha woman in Christ sins because of her fallen nature, God has made provision (1 John 1:9). God has given the Holy Spirit to aid believers in the process of sanctification.

Glorification is God's ultimate deliverance of the alpha woman in Christ from sin's presence. Glorification will not be actualized until the Lord returns for His children (1 Cor. 15:51-57). While we are living on this earth, we will always be in the presence of sin. But those who have trusted in Christ will one day be free from sin completely.

An alpha woman in Christ personal response to God's action is also of utmost importance in salvation:

- She must know who Christ is, what He has done, and what He is able to do.
- She must have a conviction that this knowledge about Christ is true.
- She must act upon that knowledge and conviction, trusting in Christ daily.

An alpha woman in Christ must have a personal encounter with Christ, surrendering her life to the Lord. At this point, salvation or "deliverance" occurs. From this point throughout eternity, the power of Christ in the woman is greater than the power of sin over the woman (2 Tim 1:12), and Christ, in turn, covers her sins by having paid the penalty for those sins through His death on the Cross. She then is challenged to live for Him and grow in His grace.

Serving in Christ

Judge, prophetess, handmaiden, missionary, queen, and businesswoman, these are a few of the ministries God had given women throughout biblical history. As "heirs of God, and joint heirs with Christ" (Rom. 8:17) and members of "the body of Christ" (1 Cor. 12:27), every alpha in Christ receives God's gifts to be used for His glory. The possibilities are as limitless as the needs of the world.

Jesus speaks each woman's name as He did that of Mary in the garden following His resurrection (John 20:11-18). When an alpha woman in Christ's response is as loving as Mary's, Jesus answers as He did to Mary with a mission and message: "Go to my brethren, and say unto them, 'I ascend unto my Father, and your Father; and to my God, and your God'" (John 20:17).

Jesus' desire is that each woman yield herself to Him in utter dependence, recognizing that "without me ye can do nothing" (John 15:5), and relying on His Spirit to fulfill the special ministry He selects for her. A ministry appropriate to her talents and effective in her generation. God challenges each of us as He did Queen Esther, "Who knoweth whether thou art come to the kingdom for such a time as this?" (Esth. 4:14).

Each woman is hand-picked by God, situated in Christ's body just as He desires, and is indispensable in reaching her particular sphere of influence for Christ. If a woman feels inadequate for the ministry task the Lord reveals to her , she need only remember Jesus' words, "My grace is sufficient for thee: for my strength is made perfect in weakness" (2 Cor. 12:9).

Chapter 2
Born to Lead

When a woman is born to lead, she is a decision maker who is committed to her goals and dreams. She may be opinionated and unafraid to speak her mind, but she is considerate, open-minded, and respectful of others. She is always ready to learn and willing to take on any challenge. Most importantly, she is dedicated to growing as a person, as a valuable and contributive member of society. She knows how important it is to serve. Women are natural leaders because we carry influence, rather we are on the front lines making decisions or behind the scenes with our influence. Our hands are in everything that is why it is important to have the right foundation to stand on so that things will not crumble around you. In every aspect of this world, you can smell the scent of a woman in the lives of children, businesses, and through man.

Bible Reference
Judges 5:7 Deborah the inhabitants of the villages ceased, they ceased Israel, until that I Deborah arose, that I rose a mother in Israel.

Deborah appears to have been a homemaker at the time she is selected for service to her country. Having no noble lineage, she is identified simply as "the wife of Lapidoth." Yet Deborah was the only woman in Scripture elevated to high political power by the common consent of her peers. Though her homemaking responsibilities may well have taken a backseat during her service to her country, she described herself as "a mother in Israel" (Judges 5:7) before she became a judge. Whether this is reference to her own offspring or an expression of her spiritual motherhood toward every son and daughter of Israel, is irrelevant.

In spiritually parched Israel, characterized by rejection of God and by a determination among the people for each to do things her own way (Judges 17:6; 21:25), Deborah was first a counselor, as she displayed her leadership under a large palm tree near her home by discussing and suggesting solutions to the people with problems. The civil court system was incompetent; the military was too weak to defend national borders; the priesthood of what had been a theocracy was powerless and ineffective. Normal life was no longer possible, and consequently Deborah became judge and finally a deliverer of her people in time of war.

In this area the despised King Jabin was harassing the Israelites. Deborah summoned Barak, from the tribe of Naphtali on the northern border, and ordered him to recruit an army of ten thousand men from his own tribe and the neighboring tribe Zebulun.

Barak wavered, insisting that Deborah accompany him for the task (Judges 4:8). She not only joined the drive to raise an army but also suggested their strategy. God had spoken in the past through His leaders Moses and Joshua, and now He was speaking through Deborah. Yahweh came to her aid with a violent thunderstorm (Judges 5:4). In a mini-play of the crossing of the Red Sea, the horse-drawn chariots of the enemy stumbled.

The destruction of the Canaanites power was immortalized in one of the finest specimens of Hebrew poetry by Deborah and Barak, as they pictured in a song of praise the events which led to victory for the people (Judges 5). Long before Deborah exercised her uncommon leadership and decision-making skills to save her nation in a time of trouble, she was a homemaker a wife of Israel. Her compassion had been awakened by the killings suffered by her people. She arose to make herself available, and she was victorious as she herself trusted God, then inspired others within her sphere of influence with that same trust.

Deborah carried the attributes of "The Alpha Woman."
Conscience Right or Wrong

Conscience is a universal, innate, God-given capacity to distinguish between right and wrong (Romans 2:14, 15). It has two functions: to urge an individual to do what is perceived to be right; and subsequently to commend or condemn, depending on whether the person did what was perceived as right. A person who has a "good" and "pure" conscience consistently and genuinely acts in conformity with an inner set Godly standards (2 Corinthians 1:12, 1 Timothy 1:5, 19; 3:9).

Conscience can be distorted, moreover, while the inner set of standards will be accurate if it is based on biblical truth, the conscience will be unreliable if faulty standards have been consistently presented to it as being true. The old saying, "Let your conscience be your guide," will only be true if your principles are infused with Godly principles.

Self-Control

Self-discipline is essential to personal development, spiritual growth, and Christian service. In some cases self-discipline does not just happen or appear as a natural trait. Alpha women must practice self-control in order to lead disciplined lives. For the alpha women, God's unlimited power can be added to limited human willpower to develop divine discipline. Divine discipline requires a personal action to receive the Holy Spirit's power.

Alpha women must learn to discipline both outward behaviors and inward feelings in order to be Godly. Words and actions as well as thoughts and passions must be acceptable to God (Psalm 19:14). A disciplined life involves a genuine, personal commitment to obey God's statutes, frequently it requires lifestyle changes. God's supernatural power is added to personal willpower as alpha women practice His presence, receive His power, and seek His joy.

The acceptance by affirmation from and accountability to other people also help an alpha woman develop self-control. Divine discipline can effect change in other ways as well. Scripture teaches that self-control is the crowning fruit of Holy Spirit (Galatians 5:22). Without self-control, the alpha woman has little opportunity to experience fully the blessings of God.

Wisdom Personified

Wisdom together with the virtuous wife (Prov.31) and the adulteress of folly (Prov. 5-7), is one of three dominate personifications in the Book of Proverbs. This book does not present a literal woman or goddess but is a means of picturing the contrast between good and evil and between wisdom and folly. This divine attribute and activity is personified as a dignified and noble woman who is warm, caring, and competent. She offers life with long-term satisfaction (Prov. 1:33; 8:34, 35). In contrast, her rival or "counter-wisdom," called "folly" (Prov. 15:21), provides immediate gratification but ultimate ruin.

Wisdom pleads with her hearers, begging them to follow her and learn how to take their knowledge about God and apply it to their lives in a practical and successful way (Prov. 8:1-11). She sets forth her virtues and her rewards. She is incomparable, better than rubies (Prov. 8:11); her instructions more precious than silver and her knowledge exceeding the worth of choice gold (Prov. 8:10). Excellent things from her lips lead to life, and her followers are blessed materially and spiritually (Prov. 8:17-21).

After specifying why wisdom and not folly is the appropriate choice, wisdom invites all who wish to sit at her banquet, to eat of the fruits of wisdom, to forsake foolishness, and to go in the way of life and understanding (Prov. 9:1-6). The shining and winsome Godliness of wisdom set against the dark and evil seductiveness of the adulteress shows the path of wisdom in all its beauty. Wisdom, in fact, foreshadows the divine wisdom found in Jesus Christ (Col. 1:9, 16-18).

Chapter 3
She Lives with Purpose

Not one day goes by that she does not know exactly what she is going to get out of that day. She lives with purpose and has clear goals for all areas of her life. The physical, mental, and spiritual goals she set for herself are more than just things she wants to accomplish, they are achievements that define her and therefore she pours her heart into them. She perseveres regardless of the circumstances or trials that come with achieving goals. She knows that it is only through God and hard work that she can continue to be the masterful woman she is.

Bible Reference:
Eve: The Creation of the Woman

No one loses value in humbly assuming the role of helper. As a "help meet" to the man, the woman became his partner spiritually in the overwhelming task of obedience to God and dominion over the earth. She was also to be a vital part of extending the generation (Gen. 1:28). The woman as ultimate friend to the man, would bring him comfort and fellowship (Gen. 2:23, 24). No one else could encourage and inspire him as she was created to do. Designed as the perfect counterpart for the man, the woman was neither inferior nor superior, but she was alike and equal to the man in her personhood while different and unique in her function. Man and woman were both created in God's image. Just as man was formed from earth, woman was formed from man. She corresponds perfectly to the man, the same flesh and blood, and in "the image of God" just as man, equal to him in every way (Gen.1:27). By the creative act itself, she is inseparably linked to the man. The unity of the race is certain (Gen. 1:27, 28); the woman's dignity and worth is confirmed (Gen. 2:22); the foundation of Christian marriage is set forth in an unforgettable way.

The woman was not an afterthought. The man was designed and created physically, emotionally, socially, and spiritually with her coming creation planned and assured. As a matter of fact, God said that the man "alone" was not good; he needed the woman. God made man from "the dust of the ground," but He made the woman from "one of the ribs" of the man.

God uses Adam to express the uniqueness of the woman in a unique composition on words. The language itself even reflects the unity God planned between the man and the woman. The expression "bone of my bones, and flesh of my flesh" happens somewhere else in the Old Testament as a manifestation of blood relationship. Even though Adam's mentioning of the woman in itself involves his authority over her, the act of assigning a name is significant and imply both authority and responsibility. The woman's name is a recognition of her origins, in the same way that Adam's name acknowledges his creation from the earth (Gen. 2:19). Eve carried the attributes of "The Alpha Woman."

The Mother of All Living Eve

Adam was given supervision over the creation, but God declared he will not live alone. The woman was created to heighten the man's creative work (Gen. 2:18-24). Eve was an indispensable part of God's plan. Both Adam and Eve, made "in the image God," stood as His representatives in the world to care for all He put under their dominion.

Purity and innocence were shattered, however, when the serpent entered the scene. Eve chose to believe Satan's lie. She was free to put her will above God's will, and she did. When she offered the fruit to her husband, he, too, disobeyed. In the New Testament, Paul clarified their actions, saying that Eve was deceived; whereas Adam ate with full knowledge of wrongdoing (2 Corinthians 11:31; 1 Timothy 2:14). Then, filled with guilt, the couple hid from God, fashioning fig leaf coverings to hide their shame. Not only had they broken their relationship with God, but also they had broken their relationship with one another, and with all generations to come, and even with the world and nature over which they were to rule. God cursed the serpent and the ground for man's sake, and He prophesied sorrow, toil, and death for the first couple. Pain for the woman would come in giving birth and rearing children and in her relationship to her husband. She would resist his leadership just as his rule over her would be destroyed (Genesis 3:16).

Evicted from her lovely home, Eve conceived and bore two sons, although her joy at their birth was changed by the heartache predicted by God. Cain murdered his brother in defiance of God's command concerning sacrifices, and God banished him. Eve was left childless until God's grace once again appeared in the form of another son, Seth, who became an ancestor of the Messiah.

Eve stands as an epitome of womanhood. Although created in God's image (Genesis 1:27), she exercised her will to disobey the Creator (Genesis 3:6), daring to challenge His authority. Disobedience was not in itself a motive but presupposed the motive. Her temptation was not merely to disobey but ultimately to have her own way or to get possession of what she wanted. As a daughter, every woman bears her likeness. Eve voices an early warning to every woman to follow the path of obedience and a resounding note of hope for women when they fail; she encountered God's justice, but she also experienced His grace (Romans 5:18, 19).

Prayer: God-Authorized Purposes

Prayer is the opportunity God gives His children to become intimately acquainted with Him. As a conversation with God, prayer enables us believers to build a personal relationship with the Lord. Prayer is an expression of believers dependence on God and, at the same time, an affirmation of God's promise to the redeemed for spiritual power.

The primary purpose of prayer is to seek God's will (1 John 5:14). Jesus in His model prayer told His disciples to ask according to the will of God (Matthew 6:10). When an alpha woman talks to the Father, each request for help and every desire for guidance should be asked in the name of Jesus. All of the conditions related to prayer are bound up in this phrase, "according to His will."

Prayer provides an opportunity for adoration, praise, thanksgiving, confession of sin, and requests for self and for others. Numerous formats for prayer are possible; prayer is as unique as each person. All prayer has a central purpose: the opportunity to express yourself fully and honestly to the Lord, to listen for His reply more often in form of insight, assurance, and joy, and to participate in the "mystery" of seeing God's purposes on this earth accomplished.

God's Will Conforming to His Purpose

An alpha woman seeks God's will and asks for God's wisdom when she is facing a major decisions. She must pray about decisions especially life decisions such as "Where shall I go to college?" "Should I marry this man?" "Should I bring my ailing parents to live in my home?" Such decisions have serious consequences, and they deserve the prayerful seeking of God's perfect wisdom. But knowing God's will does not happen solely in prayer. It also requires commitment to knowing His Word.

The Bible teaches that realizing or proving God's will is the result of habitually conforming your thinking and behavior to God's Word over a lifetime. As a Christian alpha woman reads the Bible day by day, her mind is renewed with a new way of thinking about life. Worldly ideas, attitudes, and prejudices are replaced by thoughts that conform to God's ways. This process takes time, and there are no shortcuts. The transformation is never complete until death.

The alpha woman who has an ongoing fellowship with the Lord through His Word comes to decisions equipped with a biblical informed way of thinking. Knowing God's will at major decision points is much easier if you are seeking God's will every day in Bible reading and prayer.

Chapter 4
She Is Not Afraid to Be Alone

You are not defined by romantic relationships. You know what you are capable of accomplishing with or without love in your life. In fact, sometimes you are way more productive when you are alone; so really the break-up was a blessing in disguise. You now have time to read all the books that have been collecting dust on your book shelf, or catch up with old friends. In regards to the boy? He will be replaced with a man.

Bible Reference:
Hagar: Rejected but Not Abandoned

The Egyptian maidservant Hagar was acquired by Sarai (Sarah) when she and Abram, together with his nephew, moved from Canaan to Egypt to escape a famine. In ancient Near Eastern households, the rank of personal maidservant to the master's wife reflected honor, obedience, and trustworthiness. However, the position stripped Hagar of all personal rights, making her totally subject to Sarai's every wish. Because Sarai was sterile, Hagar's surrogate maternity was perfectly legal, though a clear violation of God's law (Genesis 2:24) and evidence of a lack of faith on the part of Abram and Sarai. Psychologically and emotionally, Hagar changed radically with her pregnancy. Sarai responded to Hagar's pride and self-importance with the vindictive accusation against her husband, who insisted that Sarai assume full responsibility for her maid. Because of Sarah's mistreatment, Hagar ran away.

To this fugitive slave, God revealed Himself ("Thou God seest me," Genesis 16:13). In tender grace, He met her immediate need and allowed her to experience His presence. Hagar's legacy speaks emotionally to the growing number of disadvantaged and dispossessed women. Under no circumstance can they escape God's watch-care. As God provided for Hagar, He can and will provide for every woman. Twice the Angel of the Lord came to her aid (Genesis 16:7; 21:17). He was also involved with Hagar and her son in times of crisis and in the times in between (Genesis 21:20).

Throughout Hagar's life, she experienced estrangement and prejudice as a foreigner, hardship and abuse as a servant, grief and abandonment as an unwed pregnant woman, and hopeless despair on two occasions as she faced imminent death. Yet despite all these difficulties, Hagar responded to the God who addressed her. She did not het compensation from Sarah and Abraham; her life was never easy, but God did reward her. In the all-seeing God, Hagar found refuge in life.

Hagar carried the attributes of "The Alpha Woman."
Singleness: Many Opportunities

Singleness is a permanent state in life for some people and a temporary state in life for most. Adam was created by God and knew an experience of solitude in the garden before God created Eve. Most teenager, young adults, divorcees, and single moms experience a similar period of aloneness. The response of faith is to see singleness as a call to a committed life, not a lonely life. Made in the image of God (Genesis 1:26), the single woman ideally lives in a covenant relationship with God and is called to develop her gifts – human, spiritual – to contribute to the building-up of the church (1 Corinthians 12:7).

The single woman is called to develop a deep love relationship with the Lord and to channel her love in pure, productive, and generous ways to the benefit of others. A vital spiritual life can be her anchor for chastity and a source of stability in an evil and perverse generation (Luke 9:41; 11:29).

The single woman can experience great freedom to devote herself to work, friendship, and service, all of which can contribute greatly to the church and the extension of God's kingdom on earth. The single woman has an opportunity to give unique level of service to those in need a level of service that is unfettered and "without distraction" (1 Cor. 7:35). A generous willingness to assist others can lead to happiness and fulfillment for the single woman. A spirit of generous service, which can be a tremendous witness to the power of God, is a gift to be sought from God.

Freedom: No More Bondage

In both Old and New Testaments, freedom refers to liberation from slavery, whether in a socio-political sense (Joseph's imprisonment, Genesis 39:20-23), a spiritual sense (Galatians 4:21-5:15), or with regard to our mortality (Hebrew 2:15). Given this, our freedom, whether political or spiritual, depends on God's initiative (Micah 6:4; Romans 8:2). When Adam and Eve sinned, God came to them (Genesis 3:8) with the promise of freedom from sin's curse (Genesis 3:15).

The promise was fulfilled when God sent His Son to be the Way to eternal freedom (Luke 4:18, 19). We do not have to be slaves of sin (John 8:34), for the Truth (that is, Christ) can make us free if we will accept the price of deliverance (John 8:31, 32). We are freed from sin's bondage for a purpose: to become "servants of God" (Romans 6:22). We are free from the judgment of ourselves and others (Romans 5:9) and, at the same time, free for service to Him and others (Galatians 5:13, 14). Ultimate freedom that is, being ransomed from the slavery of sin, is vital to any understanding of redemption through the blood of Christ (Romans 6:15-23).

Chapter 5
She Understands the Importance of Balance

She understands that she needs balance in all aspects of her life: physical, mental, and spiritual. She is committed to thorough work in each of these areas to better herself and live life to the fullest. She embraces the importance of believing in something greater than herself in order to truly be fulfilled. She understands that what she puts in her body is exactly what she will get out. Therefore, she takes care of her body as if it was an ancient temple or one of the seven world wonders, which, if we are being honest, it truly is. Lastly, she does not stop developing herself intellectually, ever. It is her knowledge and wisdom of life that intrigues people, but more importantly it is what drives her to face life with courage and boldness.

Fatigue Refueling for Renewed Service

Fatigue can make a nag of anyone! Nothing goes further to make an alpha woman in Christ less able to cope with unruly children, household, or job crises, and thousands of mundane irritations. Scripture offers ways for alpha women in Christ to reduce fatigue and avoid weariness.

- Support from an understanding husband or close friends helps you handle pressure and stress more effectively. Knowing that someone not only knows about the burden but comes alongside to help you bear up under the load (Is. 50:4; Gal. 6:2) makes every crisis more tolerable.
- Alpha women in Christ are refreshed and invigorated by being able to walk away from burdens even for a few hours. Such times for yourself can provide renewal of energies and revival of spirit and can produce creativity and re-create productivity (Eccl. 5:18).

- Alpha women in Christ need to guard against over-commitment. Even good and Godly pursuits must be weighed against the purposes of God (Heb. 12:1). You must learn to say "no," determine to slow your frantic pace, resist the temptation to add more and more to your schedule. Busyness is not necessarily Godliness. Perhaps your "R and R" should become Reprioritizing responsibilities (Matt. 6:33) and Rethinking free time (Eccl. 3:1-8).

Being tired is a physical affliction. Being weary, on the other hand, is a spiritual attitude that results in part from blaming God for your own sinfulness. Life will never free you from fatigue, but fatigue can bring you to the point of setting aside the mundane cares of the world in order to open your heart and soul to the Lord (Eccl. 12:12).

God can use fatigue:

1. to cause you to look to Him for satisfaction (Is. 28:12, 13),
2. to administer correction (Heb. 12:5) as He pulls back His hand of strength to force your body to slow down for refueling,
3. to prepare you for a greater challenge (Jer. 12:5).

God has promised to satisfy fully the weary soul and replenish faithfully the sorrowful heart (Jer. 31:25). Sometimes that means, "He maketh me to lie down" (Ps. 23:2). Physical frailties may cause you to miss earthly fun and fellowship, but spiritual resources will enable you to grow stronger on the bed of affliction.

Bible Reference:
Rebekah: A Woman of Faltering Faith

Rebekah would certainly rank among the most appealing of the young women in Scripture. She is pictured as chaste and beautiful (Genesis 24:16), courteous and helpful, industrious, hospitable, as well as responsive and trusting. She was chosen as the intended bride for Isaac. Family ties were obviously close, for Rebekah's first response was to tell the women in her household all about her encounter at the well. For a girl to be chosen for marriage to a wealthy relative was indeed considered a blessing of God. Her father and brother knew also that this was from God but the choice to leave home was hers to make, reflecting the sovereignty that young women in her culture enjoyed.

Rebekah volunteered a lowly service, which opened to her a lofty destiny as God worked His plan for her life through her mundane daily responsibilities. Her courage and faith motivated her to venture from the known and familiar (family and friends) to the unknown (a new life in strange land). God rewarded Rebekah's faithfulness with a monogamous marriage, which began with romance and loving affection (Genesis 26:8), and in answer to Isaac's prayer for his wife's fertility, God removed her barrenness with the birth of twins, Esau and Jacob (Genesis 25:21).

In later years, Rebekah's weakness became clear at two points: the lack of reverence and respect for her husband and his leadership, and the exhibition of favoritism concerning her sons, which brought into the home rivalry, deceit, and contention (Genesis 25:28), (Proverbs 28 Favoritism). Rebekah's unwavering faith for her youth faltered, and she took into her own hands the direction of the future of her sons. Maybe her own discernment for her sons that is recognizing Esau as worldly and adventuresome (Genesis 26:34, 35) and Jacob as having more potential for spiritual sensitivity (Genesis 25:31) or her own empathy toward one son over the other (Genesis 25:8) or even strong faith in God's revealed plan (Genesis 25:23) motivated her own deceitful acts.

In any case, the deceiving of her husband was without excuse and her poor example to her sons was a far-reaching tragedy (Genesis 27:12, 13). Even if her motive was pure, her action was wrong. She paid a bitter price in living out her final years in separation from the son whose presence she desired, in alienation from the son who would ever remember his mother's deception toward him, and in broken fellowship from a husband who had loved her devotedly.

Rebekah carried the attributes "The Alpha Woman."
Priorities: Planning Your Days

Often women are overwhelmed by too many things to do (Luke 10:40) because there are many good choices concerning how to apportion time (Ecclesiastes 3:1-8). To set priorities is to determine what is important to you and how your time is to be apportioned that is, who and what will take precedence over other parts of life.

Scripture contains guidelines for God's order (Psalm 119:105, 130):

- Your personal relationship to Jesus Christ (Matthew 6:33; Philippians 3:8);
- Your commitment to home and family especially spouse and children (Genesis 2:24; Psalm 127:3; Ephesians 5:22, 25; 6:4; 1 Timothy 3:2-5; 5:8; 1 Peter 3:7) and even to the extended family, as so beautifully portrayed in the relationship between Ruth and Naomi (Ruth 1:16, 17);
- Your responsibility to employer and tasks assigned (1 Thess. 4:11, 12); and
- Your service to God through ministries in the church and involvement in the community.

Once alpha women have these divinely appointed criteria in mind, she is ready to sort out the opportunities that come (Psalm 32:8) and move forward in the most effective and productive management of time and resources. A very practical way of accomplishing this: list all the tasks before the task before you, consider each prayerfully as to merit and timeliness (Col 2:5), arrange them in order of importance, then proceed to do the most important things first (1 Cor14:40).

To be consistent in the priorities, consider these admonitions: assign God first place (Matt. 6:33); consult with the Father regularly in your quiet (Psalm 55:17; Luke 5:15, 16); examine your own heart (Eccl. 3:1); and keep yourself spiritually fit (Is. 30:15). Jesus met with the Father in intensive prayer and meditation to determine His priorities and to prepare Himself for each day (Luke 5:15, 16).

Put people before things (2 Cor. 8:5). Do not limit your investment in those you love, and others who cross your path, to money and gifts. Look for ways to invest yourself, your time, and your energies. Family must be more important than occupation since Scripture clearly states that there is no success if the family is lost (1 Tim. 3:5; 5:8; Titus 2:4, 5). Sometimes you must say "no," as did even Jesus when some seemingly good requests for His time did not fit the overall plan for His ministry (Luke 4:42, 43). The underlying principle in determining priorities is always that spiritual values must overshadow worldly pursuits (2 Cor. 4:18).

Goal-Setting: Plotting a Course

Goals are dreams with a deadline. In life's pursuits, you either move ahead of find yourself falling back; there is no middle ground! Some goals express good desires but cannot be measured and have no deadlines and are not achievable. Meaningful vision and realistic goals must include: an explanation of the goal (what will it take to reach that goal?), and a date for completion (what is the deadline?).

The ardent and relentless pursuit of a goal was important to Paul! He spoke of pressing "toward the mark for the prize" (1 Cor. 9:24, 25). In both cases, therefore, Paul was speaking of achieving that which is imperishable: the crown that belongs to those who answer the upward call of God in Christ Jesus. The Lord is not at all opposed to your achievement. He simply calls upon you to direct your achievement toward right and eternal things!

Biblical guidelines determine goals (1 Cor. 10:31). All goals must be consistent with the written Word of God (2 Tim. 3:14-17) and like-minded with Jesus Christ (Phil. 2:5). Goal-setting is appropriate for any age from youth through adulthood (1 Tim. 4:12-16), for all God-ordained relationships, and in all areas of life. Certain commitments are involved in setting goals: Priorities must be specific or measurable (Heb. 6:10); goals should be realistic (Phil. 3:13, 14); a plan must be developed to get the work done (1 Cor. 9:24-27); time must be set aside to complete the task (Acts 20:24); and evaluation of the goal reached ought to be included (2 Tim 4:7).

To accomplish an ultimate purpose or goal, steps are important. You first ask for direction from God (Prov. 3:5, 6). This establishes objectives for what is to be done (Psalm 37:23, 24) and determines a program for how you are going to accomplish your goal (Prov. 16:9). You must schedule when you are going to do what God has put in your heart to do (1 Chr. 12:32) and budget how much time and money is required. An alpha woman's ultimate goal is always to please God. Discover His priorities (Matt. 22:36-40); study His principles (Ps. 119:105); determine His plans (Ps. 16:7-11); note His way of evaluating progress (Gal. 6:3, 4); remember His promise for help (Phil. 1:6); commit to His way of problem-solving (Ps. 37:4-9).

Chapter 6
She Embraces Change

While most people are terrified of change, the magnificent alpha woman welcomes it. She believes there is no growth without change and no change without sacrifice. For her, the opportunity for self-development is worth far more than the fear of sacrificing the comfort of what she already knows. This is truly where the beauty of the alpha woman lies, in her ability to face life and embrace the possibilities for change.

Bible Reference:
Miriam: A Natural Leader

Miriam, an intelligent child, became, with her brothers Aaron and Moses, a leader of the people of Israel. Her appearance, babysitting her little brother beside the Nile River, demonstrates her keen mind. She volunteered to find a wet nurse for the baby when the Egyptian princess expressed her intention to adopt the child, thus allowing Moses' mother, Jochebed, to nurture him. More than eighty years later, God delivered His people from the bondage of Egypt; and after the miracle of crossing the Red Sea on dry land, Miriam led the women in dancing and singing as a celebration to God. She was clearly gifted as a natural leader and was considered the foremost of all the Hebrew women, being also gifted as a musician and prophetess (Exodus 15:20). She undoubtedly was included at the council table with her brothers, and Miriam, as his older sister, may even have acted as a surrogate mother to Moses. There is no evidence in the text that she ever married. As a single woman, she committed herself to building the nation of Israel. Her career appears to be outside the home.

During tumultuous days journeying across the desert, Moses' wife became a concern for Miriam. Whether this "Ethiopian woman" who had joined the

31

group was Zipporah or a second wife, is not known (Numbers 12:1), but her presence was cause for criticism and jealousy from Miriam and Aaron. They were not concerned because of her color but because she was from a foreign land. They apparently discussed their feelings, concluding together that they as leaders were being slighted. Miriam's mistake was her sarcastic rejection of her brother's leadership.

In anger, the Lord disciplined Miriam with instant leprosy, in which it banned her from the camp (Numbers 12:10, 14). Because of the fervent prayers of her brothers, God restored her, but there is no evidence that her influence was again blessed of God. She died before reaching the Promised Land (Numbers 20:1).

The gifted woman left a caution for every female leader. God alone gives and removes both talent and importance. Miriam incurred God's displeasure when she allowed herself to challenge the authority God had given Moses. She allowed jealousy and spitefulness to rob her of fulfillment in her later years.

Miriam carried the attributes of "The Alpha Woman."
Change Points of Life: Times of Transition

Change is an inevitable part of life! While knowledge, experience, and routine foster security, the uncertainty of change is uncomfortable for many people. When circumstances are changing, alpha women can depend on God for strength, guidance, and constancy. He never changes (Heb. 1:10-12). In times of transition, alpha women can trust a sovereign and loving God to order all the events in our lives according to His purposes (Rom. 8:28).

Every life includes nearly constant contact with change: marriage, career, children, illness, relocations, divorce, and retirement. Some changes are voluntary; others are forced by circumstances. Some changes being joy; others, sorrow and confusion. All changes can become positive, strengthening experiences for those under God's authority.

Alpha women respond to life's changes in different ways. Sometimes there is fear about the unknown. Often women lack self-confidence in times of transition. Others experience frustration, loneliness, and pain. The antidote for these feelings is faith and active obedience. Alpha women in Christ are challenged to accept the reality of change and provide words of encouragement to those experiencing change. The study of Scripture is especially important when facing change. Inner strength from God during times of distress results in God's richest blessings forever (2 Cor. 4:7-18). Change can be a gift from God to heighten, deepen, and widen your personal relationship with the Lord. Changes in life are cause to remember that God is faithful yesterday, today, and forever (Heb. 13:8).

Providence: Patient Waiting

The theme of God's providential care of His created order is woven throughout Scripture. In the Sermon on the Mount, Jesus assured His hearers of His presence in the midst of their trials (Matt. 6:25-34). God's eternal and unfailing purpose is to sustain and direct His created beings (Matt. 6:10) from the beginning of creation into eternity (John 5:17). He has shown His providential care again and again (2 Tim. 1:12), extending it from the least to the greatest, covering the sinner and the saved.

Esther was simultaneously the humble Jewess, honoring her husband, and the queen of Persia, delivering her people. The God who controlled the cruel and despotic Ahasuerus of Persia has ultimate power over every situation. God's control is all-inclusive and absolutely certain, but at the same time every individual is responsible for her decisions and actions. Still, no one can defeat the plans of God since all actions are included in His active or permissive will.

Alpha women in Christ are not under the tyranny of blind fate or an inviolable law of cause and effect, which by definition would seem to imply that there is a realm into which God cannot enter (Prov. 16:33). The events of our universe are ordered by a compassionate, gracious, long-suffering, faithful God (Ps. 16:9-11). God has not promised that everything happening to us will be what we consider good. Therefore, when tragedy strikes, the alpha women in Christ have only to wait patiently for His hour of redemption. God is able to cause even unfortunate happenings to work for good to those who love the Lord (Rom. 8:28). Nothing can happen to us apart from God's knowledge, presence, and love so that even in the most desperate circumstances, we can be assured that God is working on our behalf for our eternal good. God is for us; He is not against us (Rom. 8:31, 32). In the tension between blessings and adversity, alpha women in Christ recognize their complete dependence upon Him, as well as His sovereignty over their own decisions and actions.

Chapter 7
She Knows How to Love

Some people may argue that as an alpha woman, she is self-sufficient and have no capacity for love, they could not be further from the truth. Instead, people fail to see that she thoroughly understands her worth and therefore accurately guards her heart until she finds worthy individuals to pour her love on. When she does, the love-fest is unconditional, faithful, and true. While everyone else is waiting to get swept off their feet, she is not afraid to make the first move and fight for what she believes is rightly hers, her one true love.

Love: More Than a Feeling

Throughout Scripture we are assured of God's love and reminded that the proof of God's endless love is that Chris died for us (Romans 5:8; 1 John 4:9, 10). But love is not simply meant to make us feel good rather to motivate us to respond in ways that make us emulate His goodness. Love sometimes demands that we act in very practical and even uncomfortable ways.

- Love is not optional (1 John 3:11, 23, 4:11). We are commanded to love one another.
- Love is demonstrative (1 John 3:14; 4:7, 20). Our love for God is shown to the degree we show to others.
- Love is active, an act of the will (1 John 3:17). We are commanded to do the acts of love. If we shut our eyes to the needs of others, our love for God is called into question.
- Love is responsive (1 John 4:19). We are able to love because we have been and are loved by God. This love causes us to respond lovingly to others (1 John 4:21).

God: He Is Love

Love is not a definition of God. God is infinitely more but God is the definition of love. Without Him, love does not exist (John 3:16; 1 John 4:8-10); Biblical love (Agape) is active, yet selfless. Though most graphically and fully illustrated in God's love for us, agape love is also God's pattern for our love for Him (1 John 4:19) and for our love for one another (Ephesian 5:25; 1 Peter 1:22). Its basis is God's deliberate, active, sacrificial giving of His Son for our redemption. To be loved by God means that He has set His sights on us and is actively wooing us toward Him at all times.

God's love is self-starting (1 John 4:10), indestructible (Romans 8:38, 39), undeserved (Romans3:23), compassionate (Isaiah 49:15), constant (Jeremiah 31:3), immeasurable (Ephesian 3:18, 19), voluntary (Romans 5:8), and a gift (John 3:16). He did not begin loving at the Cross, nor will He love us more tomorrow than He does today. There is nothing we can do, think, or say that will change His love because there are no surprises for God. He knows us totally and loves us anyway (Psalm 139:1-5). The goal of God's love is to have us with Him throughout eternity (1 John 4:16). He presented and made possible the accomplishment of this goal through Jesus and His sacrifice on the Cross (John 1:14-18).

Love Is an Action

Love is an action word, indicating conscious acts on behalf of a beloved. Biblical love seems to demand going beyond merely a particular behavior to include a certain inner attitude, that is, a positive inner response. The attributes of love reflect both feelings and loving acts (1 Cor. 13:4-8). True love is characterized as:

- Patient and slow to anger
- Kind and gentle to all
- Unselfish and giving
- Truthful and honest
- Hopeful and encouraging
- Enduring without end

Love is an attribute carried by "The Alpha Woman."

35

Chapter 8
She Is Very Much Misunderstood

Society has this incessant need of fitting her into a mold and quite frankly that does not work with her. She is unapologetic about her opinions. She is unrestrained about her beliefs. She believes in what she believes in, and there is very little others can do to change her mind once it has been made up. Because of her strong sense of self and her uncontainable confidence, she is very much misunderstood. Society cannot understand how it is possible for a woman to be so bold, so courageous, and so thoroughly and magnificently breathtaking. She must never feel like she must change to fit someone else's opinion of her.

Bible Reference:
Ruth 1 – Naomi: A Wise Mother-in-Law

During the time of the judges, approximately 1200 B.C a famine in the region of Bethlehem caused Abimelech to take his wife Naomi and their two sons to the green fields of Moab, east of the Dead Sea. Shortly after arriving, Abimelech died, and Naomi was left as an alien to work in a nation that practiced polygamy and idol worship.

In time, her two sons chose wives, Ruth and Orpah, before whom Naomi continued to live a pious life of dedication to Yahweh (God). As a widow and a single parent, she demonstrated inner strength; when both of her sons died, she faced her destitution with resoluteness, determined to return to her home in Israel. Her life had been disappointing, but her faith was intact. Consequently, she insisted that her daughters-in-law return to their mothers' homes. Both of them resisted, but eventually Orpah, the widow of Chilion, returned. Ruth vowed to accompany Naomi back to Jerusalem, renouncing her own family and religion. Naomi learned that even in the midst of greatest suffering and adversity, God is good and full of mercy.

Naomi lives as a true heroine. Her unfaltering faith during years of adversity and her careful tutoring of her young protégé Ruth under difficult circumstances exemplify a woman of deep spiritual understanding.

Naomi carried the attributes of "The Alpha Woman."
Emotions: Expressing What Is Within

Emotions are at the core of our being and reflect one profound aspect of the wonder of being made in the image of God (Num. 32:10; Is. 53:3; John 11:33). More than anything else, they reflect our attitudes and behavior. Emotions often express outwardly our innermost beliefs. For instance, if we believe in God's sovereignty and ultimate control, exchange fear and worry for peace and contentment.

God makes Himself known to us not only in truth and by decree but in the way He reveals His heart. God is passionate in His pursuit of us, and that passion is expressed in a variety of emotions: grief at the rebellion of His children (Hos. 11:8, 9), anger at their idolatry (Jer. 2:1-13), and delight upon their return to Him (Luke 15:11-32). God's longing for an unhindered relationship with His children is found all through Scripture (Jer. 17:9, 10).

Alpha women in Christ who are made in His image not only think and choose how they feel. Their personalities are interwoven with an intricate mix of mind, will, and emotions. To be able to experience pain or joy, sadness or anger is to feel alive. You not only do yourself damage and limit your potential in Christ when you deny or suppress your emotions, you reduce your understanding of who God is. Emotion that is passionate, heartfelt desire is part of the energy that bonds believers to God and to each other in a rich, meaningful way.

Emotions are a gift from God intended to compel us to take action. For example, our anger at a wrong committed against us or someone else can compel us to seek justice. As important as our emotions are, we must never be ruled by them rather, we must subject our emotions to a will that is yielded to God. All emotions are intended to be expressed in a Godly manner so as not to cause hurt to other people or result in manipulation of other people.

Emotional Healing: Restoring the Positive

Emotions are God-given, spontaneous responses to events. A person perceives an event in a particular way, and an emotion is aroused that leads to one of at least three responses: The emotion is allowed to escalate so that it becomes destructive to yourself or others; its validity is denied; or it is directed in a manner appropriate and healthy for the situation. Emotions themselves are neither good nor bad. The problem lies in the thoughts that produce emotions and in behavior resulting from emotions.

Because they are spontaneous, emotions do not last for an extended period unless they are nurtured by the mind and will. Emotions are a caution light reminding us to re-examine what we are thinking. Paul does not condemn anger (an emotion indicating a boundary has been crossed) but counsels the Ephesians to deal with it quickly. Anger, when wedded with hurt and sham, can develop into bitterness and provide fertile ground for further temptation (Eph. 4:26, 27, 31; Heb. 12:15).

When an alpha woman in Christ is shamed for having an emotional response such as fear or anger, her tendency is to protect herself by blocking these emotions from conscious awareness. She, being bound by shame, is unable to express the emotion in appropriate, healthy ways. Since emotions are interconnected, denying painful emotions also necessitates burying pleasant ones, and the result is often emotional numbness. Scripture challenges women to identify your emotions (Ps. 13:1-3; 77:1-6) and to learn how to channel them into positive behaviors. As painful memories surface, you can bring them to God for healing and restoration, allowing Him to remove the shame that has been linked to those memories.

Integrity: Singleness of Heart

Some mistakenly associate the word "integrity" only with reputation and external appearance. True integrity is a quality of character, an inward reality that refers to singleness of heart or mind, the development of a blameless character by adhering to an exemplary moral code. The biblical model of integrity is marked by several distinct features:

- Innocent actions (Gen. 20:5);
- A clear conscience (Acts 24:16, Heb. 13:8);
- Fear of God, truthfulness, and opposition to covetousness (Ex. 18:21);

- Blamelessness and uprightness (Job 2:3; Ps. 25:21);
- Righteousness (Ps. 7:8);
- Freedom from that which is shameful, crafty, or deceitful (2 Cor. 4:2);
- Refusal to serve idols (Ps. 24:3-5);
- Disassociation with evil-doers (Ps. 26:4);
- Honorable behavior (2 Cor. 8:21; 1 Pet. 2:12).

The Hebrews understood that:

- Integrity of heart guides a person into right and rewarding situations (Prov. 11:3);
- Integrity is more acceptable to the Lord than sacrifice (Prov. 21:3); and
- A person's integrity silences critics (1 Pet. 2:13-17).

Integrity provides a mind-set toward righteousness and an abiding intent to do the will of God and to walk in His ways.

Chapter 9
She Is an Uncontrollable Risk Taker

For her, there is no life without risk! What others may see as reckless, she sees as an opportunity for stepping out of her comfort zone and let her courage shine. Taking these risks in life is what drives her and keeps her focused on becoming the woman she longs to be and who God called her to be. She never conforms and always perseveres. She is simply a natural risk taker!

Bible Reference:
Ruth 1:16-18 – A Faithful Moabite

Ruth lives in history as a model of womanhood, willing in joy and confidence to break with her past on the basis of God's revelation taught to her by a loving mother-in-law. God uses the faithfulness of ordinary women to accomplish His extraordinary plans: He provided bread for the two widows through Ruth's collecting; He provided security for the young widow Ruth through her marriage to Boaz; He provided posterity for Naomi through Obed, the son born to Ruth and Boaz; God provided a great king for Israel and even the Messiah through this Gentile woman. All of this describes clear communication.

Ruth carried the attributes of "The Alpha Woman."
Boldness: A Memorial Presence

Biblical boldness describes clear communication unhindered by fear (Phil. 1:14). A woman can be frank in her speech because of confidence in her spirit (Phil. 1:20). Such determination to make your opinions known gives memorable presence and makes your influence felt. Boldness should not be equated with obnoxious or aggressive personalities. It is a gift to be sought by every believer. We ask and receive boldness from God (Acts 4:29-31). New

Testament boldness is not found in safe and secure places but rather where God's Word needs to be on the cutting edge to penetrate the hearts and minds of the individuals to whom we relate. God uses boldness for His own purpose. Our weaknesses is used by God to prove His strength (Acts 4:13). Rahab, the prostitute, acted to aid God's people and save herself and her family. Her boldness brought forgiveness for her sins and a place in the genealogy of the Messiah (Josh. 6:17, 22-25; Matt. 1:5). Abigail, the wife of an abusive husband, acted redemptive in making a bold personal appeal to David for the lives of her husband and their servants (1 Sam. 25:23-35). Ruth, the Gentile widow, accepted her mother-in-law's plan and boldly asked Boaz to be her kinsman-redeemer and become her husband (Ruth 3:1-11).

Queen Esther knew that God was in control of the king (Prov. 21:1), and she made her intercession for her people first to the Lord (Esth. 4:15, 16). She continued to be sensitive to God's timing and patiently waited for the ideal opportunity to make her bold request to Ahasuerus (Esth. 5-8). Esther did not attempt to take the authority of her husband the king, nor did she seek to deceive him or the court, nor did she devise a plan of manipulation (Esth. 5:2-8). Submission and boldness are not opposing. When boldness is founded upon unwavering confidence overwhelming opposition and receive the blessing and Favor of God.

Confidence

In the Old Testament, the words "confidence" and "assurance" are different forms of the same Hebrew word. Isaiah adds the concept of quietness, "In quietness and in confidence" (Is.30:15) we find our strength. Isaiah also tells us that "quietness and assurance" are the effect of righteousness (Is. 32:17). In the New Testament, the Greek words translated "assurance" (Col. 2:2) and "persuaded" (Rom. 8:38) convey the same idea as similar words in the Old Testament.

Assurance is not based on optimism about your own abilities. Rather it is an inward peace based on God's righteous work in you. Such confidence is not self-confidence, for that would be false security and reliance on something unreliable (Prov. 14:16; Jer. 9:23, 24). Scripture states that those who have confidence in their own strength (Is. 30:12), beauty (Ezek.16:15), or righteousness (Ezek. 33:12) are to be considered fools (Prov. 28:26). True confidence rooted in the Lord's capabilities and His relationship with His children is a quiet strength that brings "great recompense of reward" (Heb. 10:35, 36), a lasting security that is fully satisfying.

Chapter 10
She Knows That She Doesn't Know

Her wisdom and constant pursuit for knowledge have taught her that she doesn't know everything. This is what saves her and keeps her from becoming arrogant and self-absorbed. Continue to keep this in mind, knowing that there is always room to discover and learn from others. This is crucial to keep the balance in her life; especially because her natural ways are so overpowering. With time, she will learn when to step aside and let someone else shine, knowing that stepping aside won't diminish her light, instead it will enhance it even more.

Bible Reference:
Matthew 15:24 – Syrophoenician Woman

A mother's heart is one of the most potent motivators known. A Syrophoenician (or Canaanite) woman exhibited this during one of Jesus' teaching tours. We do not know her name, but we do know this mother had insight, courage, persistence, and initiative. Obviously, Jesus' reputation had reached beyond Palestine. Most likely His healing ministry had made the news in Tyre and Sidon, but few would cross cultural and religious lines to approach Him. This woman was one of the few. What motivated her to take such initiative on her own? Her mother's heart. There were at least three barriers that could have discouraged her from accomplishing her task: She was a Gentile (Matthew 15:24); she was a Canaanite; and she was a woman (John 4:27). But the magnitude of a mother's love pulled her as irresistibly as the moon pulls the tides.

This mother used a twofold approach: She acknowledged Jesus as the rightful King by calling Him Lord; and she prayed the simple prayer, "Have mercy on me"; "help me." These expressions are irresistible to God.

Her persistence during this brief encounter with Jesus revealed not only a mother's determination but also her growing faith. Notice: It was not her love for her daughter that impressed Him the most (though that surely pleased Him) but her great faith.

There is an uncanny parallel between this woman and Rahab in the Old Testament (Josh 2). Both women came from the hopelessly perverted Canaanites; both showed a strong love for family; both showed courage, persistence, and boldness by stepping away from their religious backgrounds on their own; both evaluated Israel's God and found Him superior to their gods (in fact, they gave Yahweh more credit than the Israelites did); made a commitment to Israel's God; and both received what they were seeking. God has a special understanding for the mother's heart. More than anything else, we remember this woman's persistent, even obstinate, faith.

Syrophoenician Woman carried the attributes of "The Alpha Woman."

Tears: A Cry Out from the Heart

Alpha women in Christ are brought to tears for a multitude of reasons. Tears have always been closely intertwined with the human heart and may express such diverse emotions as grief and joy. In the Old Testament, tears were often an expression of remorse (Lam. 2:18, 19). Esther wept with a troubled soul over the plight of her people (Esth. 8:3). Hannah shed tears from a heart that grieved and a soul that was bitter (1 Sam. 1:8, 10). Mary and Martha wept over the loss of their brother Lazarus (John 11:31). The sinful woman at the feet of Christ shed tears, not from remorse, anxiety, or grief, but rather in humility as a grateful response to God's mercy and love toward her (Luke 7:38-50).

All of us will experience circumstances in our lives that will move us to tears. In those times, let us hold fast to the promise that a day is coming when God will "wipe away all tears...there shall be no more...crying" (Rev. 7:17; 21:4; Is. 25:8) Until the time, may our desire be for tears of repentance, adoration, thankfulness, and joy (Ps. 6:4-8; 126:5; 2 Tim. 1:3-5).

Distress: A Time to Call upon the Lord

Many were the distresses of the psalmist. Without exceptions, however, the psalmist turned to the Lord God to be the source of his deliverance in those difficult times (Ps. 18:3, 6). Many of the psalms reflect the pattern found in Psalm:

- The psalmist declared his love for the Lord, whom he knows has proven to be sufficient.
- He called out to the Lord to save him from his enemies, confident that God heard him.
- He expressed a heartfelt longing for God's deliverance.
- He acknowledged that God is in control despite all the catastrophes he experienced.
- He remained confident even in the midst of delays that kept him from immediate deliverance.
- He glorified God when deliverance came or his enemies were defeated.

In the midst of the trials and difficulties that inevitably come, believers can be confident that they are loved, that they will be ultimately delivered, that every delay will be used to edify and make them better, and that deliverance is assured (Rom. 8:31-39).

Chapter 11
Called to Be Strong and Affirming

Being a godly alpha woman in Christ begins with the priorities nourishing your personal relationships to God (Matt. 6:33), ministering to your husband (Prov. 18:22; 19:14), nurturing your children (2 Tim. 1:5), keeping your home (Titus 2:5), then adding whatever other activities time and energy permit (Prov. 31:10-31). This passage praises a "virtuous woman" ("woman of strength") in the form of an acrostic, with each successive verse beginning with one of the twenty-two letters in the Hebrew alphabet. This divinely inspired portrait of an ideal wife includes: pleasant appearance (31:22, giving her husband a sense of pride), godly character (Prov. 31:10-12, 17, 25, 30, 31, without a materialistic mindset), efficiency in homemaking (Prov. 31:13-15, 21, 27, seeing value in the mundane household tasks), helpfulness to her husband (Prov. 31:11, 23, 28, especially when he is emotionally and spiritually drained), attentiveness to her children (Prov. 31:28, understanding the awesome task of producing the next generation), interest in her community (Prov. 31:20, 26), willingness to use energies and creativity (Prov. 31:16, 18, 19, 24), and determination to be worthy of honor and commendation (Prov. 31:28-31). These very positive qualities are contrasted with the contentious wife (Prov. 19:13, 21:9, 19) and "strange" woman elsewhere (Prov. 5:3-14, 20; 6:24-32; 7:6-27).

An alpha woman in Christ as a wife also has unique needs that are best met by her own husband:

- Spiritual leadership, including family worship of prayer and Bible study (1 Pet. 3:7)
- Personal affirmation (Eph. 5:25)
- Tender loving care, including touching, courtesies, and loving words (Prov. 5:19)

- Intimate, sensitive, and understanding communication (Song 2:16)
- Integrity worthy of respect and transparency so that nothing is hidden (Gen. 2:25)
- Provision and sustenance as well as protection (Gen. 2:15)
- Commitment of loyal devotion (Eccl. 9:9)

Scripture describes the creation of woman with the word "made" (built). God planned and supervised this "building" of the woman with the intent that she would be a "help meet for him." Unlike animals, the woman was of the same nature as the man (Gen. 2:18-23). The word "help" is also used to describe God (Ps. 33:20). It is a term of function rather than worth. A woman does not lose value as a person by humbly assuming the role of a helper. The wife then has the assignment of being her husband's helper:

1. as a spiritual partner, assisting him in obeying the Word of God and in doing spiritual ministries,
2. as counterpart in linking hands with the Creator to continue the generations,
3. as a confidant to offer comfort and fellowship (Gen. 2:23, 24), and
4. as a companion to provide encouragement and inspiration.

Counseling: Helping Others Help Themselves

Human beings were created by God with a variety of needs: physical, emotional, intellectual, psychological, and spiritual. These needs God is ready and able to supply (Phil. 4:19). We find His help in prayer, study of Scripture, guidance of the Holy Spirit ("comforter," "called alongside"), and from the counsel of godly and wise individuals whether family, friends, or professionals.

God may choose to meet a need through an individual, or people helper, within an organization or institution or through particular circumstances. When making important or life-changing decisions, an alpha woman in Christ does well to seek counsel from wise, mature Christians (Prov. 11:14). When life's needs are not met in appropriate and effective ways, mental anguish occurs. When this anguish results in serious disruptions of daily activities or damage to relationships, counseling is necessary. To seek biblical counseling is often helpful and should not bring shame or embarrassment. Christian counseling provides the individual with healing, integration, balance, and wholeness through a variety of methods but is always marked by reliance upon the Lord as the Great Physician. Jesus assured His followers of the indwelling presence of the Holy Spirit, the Comforter, the Helper, the resident Counselor for every believer. (John16:13).

Wisdom: Fear of God

Wisdom is the process of discernment in which choices are weighed and alternatives judged. For the alpha woman in Christ, choices are always to be made in keeping with God's purposes and desires. In the Old Testament, wisdom was used in a variety of ways. Its usage ranged from describing artistic skills (Ex. 36:1-3) and financial savvy (Prov. 8:18-21) to the ability to discern truth. Wisdom is regarded as being very practical in application. It flows from a reverent awe of God and a deep respect for God's Word (Prov. 1:7; 2:6). The wise person is repeatedly described as one who acknowledges, relies upon, and trusts God's superior understanding.

Wise decisions are those that keep an alpha woman in Christ from all that is wicked and perverse (Prov.2:7-9, 12). The wisdom literature of the Bible – Job, Proverbs, Ecclesiastes, and selected Psalms – contains passages that offer very practical advice and give observations about the results of wise and foolish choices. Throughout the book of Proverbs, wisdom is portrayed as a woman (Prov. 1; 8; 9). Wisdom begs and pleads for women and men to choose the way that leads to health and life, the way of fearing the Lord that brings purpose and meaning to life and the development of a living relationship with God. The wisdom of Proverbs is applied in a special way to the many relationships that woman have: wife-husband; mother-child; daughter-parent; friend-friend; employer-employee; and neighbor-neighbor.

Wisdom for the alpha woman in Christ is a knowledge of God's will that allows her to live a life that is pleasing to the Lord (Col. 1:9, 10). Wisdom is evident when an alpha woman in Christ leads a life that is marked by purity, peace, gentleness, a yielding spirit, mercy, and "good fruits, without partially, and without hypocrisy" (James 3:17). The good news throughout Scripture is that the Lord gives wisdom liberally and without reproach to all who ask Him (James 1:5, 6). So if an alpha woman in Christ asks the Lord in faith to show her what to do, what to say, and how to live, she can count on Him to reveal to her His answer.

Heroines: Role Models for Women

Nearly all human behavior is the result of imitating others. An alpha woman in Christ's role model or heroines are a good indication of the character traits that she desires in her own life and is likely to emulate. Fortunately, in Scripture, Christian women have examples of many women who exhibited great courage, faithfulness, and achievement. Women we might take as personal role models and women we might lift up to our daughters.

Above all, we are to choose for ourselves and our daughters' role model who are righteous, those who are in right standing with God (Gen: 1:26, 27), and we are expected to reflect the image of Christ (Romans 8:29). While the Bible records some examples of unrighteous lives (Heb. 4:11; 2 Peter 2:6), it has many more examples of those who lived righteous lives of faith (Phil. 3:17; 2 Thess. 3:9). Alpha women in Christ must make certain always that our role models and those our children seek to follow are women and men who give godly example in word, conduct, love, spirit, faith, and purity (1 Tim 4:12).

Hebrews 11 records the lives of a number of women and men of faith and gives instruction for modeling Godly behavior. These women and men were not always famous or highly exalted by the masses of people in their day (Heb. 11:35-38), but all had a "good report" and played a vital role in God's unfolding plan. As a whole, they displayed a good testimony, a righteous witness, useful gifts, Godly fear, absolute obedience, unfailing hope, and patient endurance.

Intuition: Wise Sensitivities

Intuition is the ability to sense something that is not readily evident to know something without deducing that knowledge through reasoning. In the Bible, this ability is called discernment:

- of spirits including discerning the purposes and truth of God and the operation of beings in the spiritual realm (1 Cor. 12:10; 1 John 4:1);
- of the human will (Heb. 4:12).

Jesus was intuitive. We are told repeatedly that in His dealings with unrighteous men, He knew "their thoughts," even though Jesus personally had no treachery and no experience with sin (Matt. 12:25; John 6:6, 64). Abigail showed discerning intuition in her evaluation of the danger to her household from David and his men and in her wise intervention to protect her husband and his property (1 Sam. 25:2-35). Intuition frequently operates at the level of motive recognizing the plans of a person's heart (Prov. 16:9). It is closely aligned with dreams, visions, and the interpretation of natural signs (Matt. 16:2-4). Discernment is regarded as a spiritual gift and, as much, is subject to verification by the Word of God through multiple witnesses (1 Cor. 12:10).

Obedience: Doing God's Will

Bible clearly commands alpha women in Christ always to obey the Lord (Deut. 4:30; 11:1-32; Dan. 7:27; Acts 5:29). Specifically, alpha women are required to hear His Word and do His Will (James 1:22). Our obedience flows out of our love for God (1 John 2:3, 4). If the alpha woman loves the Lord, she will want to serve Him; and in serving Him, she will want to obey His commandments. Acts of obedience, therefore, are to be reflective of an inner reality that we love the Lord deeply and are committed to Him completely.

Alpha women in Christ are to also obey the human authorities that the Lord has placed in our lives, recognizing that all authority flow from God and is ultimately part of His plan (Heb. 13:7, 17; 1 Pet. 2:13, 14). Scripture advocates clearly that wives submit to husbands (Eph. 5:22), children obey parents (Eph. 6:1) slaves obey masters (Col. 3:22), Christians obey church leaders (1 Thess. 5:12, 13; Heb. 13:7), and citizens obey government officials (Heb. 13:17). Obedience is not an automatic response. It must be learned, and conversely, we must teach it to our children (Deut. 6:7-9). Obedience to those in the line of authority is part of God's plan for establishing peace and security so that we might not only fulfill our own potential but effectively extend the gospel to others.

In obeying those God has placed over us in authority, an alpha woman in Christ must recognize that we are never to break the commandments of God (see Jochebed, as well as Daniel, Shadrach, Meshach, and Abednego as examples of those who disobeyed civil authorities in their ultimate obedience to the Lord – Ex. 1:17; 2:3-10; Dan. 3:9-26; 6:13-22). We are to obey the requests of authorities that are within the bounds of righteousness, regardless of our personal desires, preferences, opinions, or perceptions, trusting the Lord to honor our obedience, to guide those in authority over us, and to deal with those authorities as He wills. The consequences of our obedience lie in His domain.

The Lord promises deliverance for our enemies (Ex. 23:22), strength, and blessings as we obey. Disobedience, on the other hand, results in disaster materially, psychologically, and spiritually. Even so, disobedience is a part of the sinful nature and is inevitable in all our lives. Israel frequently failed to hear and do God's will (Jer. 7:13; Hos. 9:17). When we disobey, we can take heart that disobedience is forgivable. The Lord offers undeserved mercy and complete forgiveness t those who confess their disobedience (Rom. 11:30-32) and make a new choice to obey.

Chapter 12
She Lives by the Fruit of the Spirit

Fruit of the Spirit is visible growth in Jesus Christ. Fruit of the Spirit is a biblical term that sums up the nine visible attributes of a true Christian life. According to King James Version of Galatians 5:22-23, these attributes are:

- love
- joy
- peace
- longsuffering
- gentleness
- goodness
- faith
- meekness, and
- temperance.

Learned in Scripture that these are not individual "fruits" from which we pick and choose. Rather, the fruit of the Spirit is one nine fold "fruit" that characterizes all who truly walk in the Holy Spirit. Collectively, these are the fruits that all alpha women in Christ should be producing in their new lives with Jesus Christ.

The fruit of the Spirit is a physical manifestation of a Christian's transformed life. In order to mature as believers, alpha women in Christ should study and understand the attributes of the nine fold fruit:

Love – "And so we know and rely on the love God has for us. God is love. Whoever lives in love, lives in God, and God in him" (1 John 4:16). Through Jesus Christ, alpha woman in Christ's greatest goal is to do all things in love.

"Love is patient, love is kind. It does not envy, it does not boast, it is not proud. It is not rude, it is not self-seeking, it is not easily angered, it keeps no record of wrongs. Love does not delight in evil but rejoices with the truth. It always protects, always trusts, always hopes, and always perseveres. Love never fails" (1 Cor. 13:4-8).

Joy – "The joy of the Lord is your strength" (Nehemiah 8:10). "Let us fix our eyes on Jesus, the author and perfecter of our faith, who for the joy set before him endured the cross, scorning its shame, and sat down at the right hand of the throne of God" (Hebrew 12:2).

Peace – "Therefore, since we have been justified through faith, we have peace with God through our Lord Jesus Christ" (Romans 5:1). "May the God of hope fill you with all joy and peace as you trust in him, so that you may overflow with hope by the power of the Holy Spirit" (Romans 15:13).

Long-suffering (patience) – We are "strengthened with all might, according to his glorious power, unto all patience and longsuffering with joyfulness" (Colossians 1:11). "With all lowliness and meekness, with longsuffering, forbearing on another in love" (Ephesians 4:2).

Gentleness – "Wherefore also we pray always for you, that our God would count you worthy of this calling, and fulfill all the good pleasure of his goodness, and the work of faith with power" (2 Thessalonians 1:11). "For the fruit of the Spirit is in all goodness and righteousness and truth" (Ephesians 5:9).

Faith (faithfulness) – "O Lord, thou art my God; I will exalt thee, I will praise thy name; for thou hast done wonderful things; thy counsels of old are faithfulness and truth" (Isaiah 25:1). "I pray that out of his glorious riches he may strengthen you with power through his Spirit in your inner being, so that Christ may dwell in hearts through faith" (Ephesians 3:16-17).

Meekness – "Bretheren, if a man be overtaken in a fault, ye which are spiritual, restore such an one in the spirit of meekness; considering thyself, lest thou also be tempted" (Galatians 6:1). "With all lowliness and meekness, with longsuffering, forbearing one another in love" (Ephesians 4:2).

Temperance (self-control) – "But also for this very reason, giving all diligence, add to your faith virtue, to virtue knowledge, to knowledge self-control, to self-control perseverance, to perseverance Godliness, to brotherly kindness, and to brotherly kindness love" (2 Peter 1:5-7).

The fruit of the Spirit should be studied by alpha women in Christ at any level of spiritual maturity.

Chapter 13
She Lives by Faith

Every word God speaks is true (John 17:17). He is unable to speak an untruth (Heb. 6:17), and He is never mistaken (Deut. 32:4). He knows all things as they really are and sees what has happened, is happening, and will happen (Is. 46:9, 10). Since He is responsible for everything all accurate knowledge comes from Him. He is the standard for all truth; He is that by which all else is measured.

Truth not only describes what He knows; it also describes all He does and says, including judgment (Is. 16:5), creation (Ps. 146:6), redemption (Ps. 31:5), and each detail of every promise He makes (Josh 23:14). Truth is so identified with God that Jesus simply states, "I am...the truth" (John 14:6), identifying Himself as the only way to the understanding of genuine truth (1 John 5:20). The fact that God is Truth is the basis of faith because the opposite of having faith in God is calling God a liar (Rom. 3:4). He is not only dependably accurate, but He is also accurately dependable.

Testing the Strengthening of Your Faith

In a sense, every day of life is a test of our relationship with God. But to each alpha woman in Christ come seasons of special joy or adversity. Both good times and bad times present opportunities for testing our trust in the Lord.

For the alpha woman in Christ, this is not like a classroom exam; God is not watching us with grade in hand, waiting to "pass" or "fail" us based on our performance. Since all have sinned, no human being on this earth could pass such test (Rom. 6:23). Testing comes through the circumstances of our lives so that we can know our own hearts more insightfully and appreciate God's grace more deeply. In such times of testing, we become aware of our thoughts, attitudes, and emotions. Through this self-awareness, God shows us where we must yet yield to Him in trusting obedience.

As the psalmist has written, when God exposes our hearts through testing, He is leading us away from the ways of the world and into the way that is everlasting (Ps. 139:23, 24). The same kinds of joy and adversity come to believers as to unbelievers. The unbeliever can make little sense of life and her response to it. The alpha woman can walk through the testing of life's joys and sorrows with full assurance that in Jesus Christ she is becoming the woman God created her to be.

Image of God: His Reflection in Us

What a magnificent concept God's creation of mankind in His image patterned after Him, mirroring a family resemblance of Him (2 Cor. 3:18). This does not pertain to the physical nature but rather to the spiritual and moral nature.

How are we like God?

- We are capable of communicating, and in so doing, we can bless or curse (James 3:9).
- We are creative, and creativity gives us joy and satisfaction (Prov. 31:13-22).
- We experience emotions and feelings; we long for relationship and fellowship (Ps. 16:11).
- We discern between right and wrong (Is. 3:18).
- We act and are responsible for our actions (John 3:18).
- We long to pursue Him. Mary sat at Jesus' feet, listening to Him. Jesus let her know that sitting at His feet was important (Luke 10:42).

Even though the original intimate relationship between God and humanity was severed by the Fall (Gen. 3:5-7), God has pursued His children down through the ages, sending His Son that we might be reconciled to Him and become His daughters and sons, His heirs (Rom. 8:14-17). His image can be reflected in us. Through Christ the image is brought back into focus so that His glory shines from the reflection.

He Is Immutable

Alpha women in Christ can be sure of God. His character, truth, ways, purposes, love, and promises never vary (Is. 46:9-11). He has never been less than what He is, nor will He be more (Mal. 3:6). People change because of inadequate ability, lack of knowledge, change of circumstances or loss interest. God lacks no ability (Gen. 18:14), He knows everything, controls everything, and is involved in everything (Is. 40:11-14).

God does nothing partially (Is. 41:4), never changes moods (Heb. 13:8), nor does He cool off in His affections (Jer. 31:3) or enthusiasm (Phil. 1:6). His attitude toward is the same as at it was in the garden of Eden, and His love is the same as it was when He displayed it on the Cross (Rom. 5:17). God never alters His plans because they are made with complete knowledge and control (Ps. 33:11). What He does in time He planned in eternity, and what He planned in eternity He carries out in time (Is. 46:9-11). God does not change because He is bigger than all causes.

Chapter 14
Prosperity More Than Possessions

God desires His children to prosper in all things (Gen. 39:3), and He promises prosperity to the Godly (Job 22:23-27). Biblical prosperity means more than financial wealth or material possessions. True prosperity is total well-being and is dependent upon a lifestyle of righteousness.

The righteous alpha women in Christ who meditate on God's Word are those who prosper abundantly (Ps. 1:1-3). Prosperity from God is reserved for those who do the will of God (Josh. 1:8), keeping His statutes, His commandments, His judgments, and His testimonies (1 Kin. 2:3). Strength and courage as well as prosperity are offered to all who fulfill statutes and judgments of the Lord (1 Chr. 22:13). The alpha women in Christ who live God's way are in position to receive God's help and blessing.

While the Lord rejoices in the prosperity of His children (Ps. 35:27, Eccl. 7:14), He also warns the alpha woman in Christ about its dangers. As God's children enjoy the blessings of a prosperous life, they naturally tend to forget the source of their blessings (Deut. 8:10-18) and begin to rely on their possessions (including intangible possessions such as family, intelligence, or innate talents) of their identity, ability, and security. Christians are reminded to recognize always that it is God who gives the power to acquire material prosperity (James 1:17).

Jesus taught that material possessions are not a measure of a person's value or spiritual worthiness (Luke 12:15). Paul warned against a pursuit of prosperity as a person's primary motive or "love" (1 Tim. 6:9, 10). Alpha women in Christ should depend entirely on the Lord to provide all their needs (Matt. 6:25, 26) and should give Him thanks as He does.

Chapter 15
Praise: Adoration of the Heart

Praising God is not something that comes naturally to anyone. Praise runs an aggravating interference pattern against your nature. Occasionally, praise feels more like a duty, an obligatory lip service performed at the opening of prayer. With persistence every alpha woman in Christ can learn to praise God in all things.

Who is to praise God? All of God's people, all of creation (Ps. 145:4, 5; Is. 55:12). Where do you praise God? Praise is fitting wherever you are (Ps. 96:3). How do you praise God? Praise is expressed through words and music (Ps. 33:1-3). When do you praise God? God should be praised at all times (Ps. 34:1). What do you praise God for? God is praised for His greatness (Ps. 150:2). Why do you praise God? God is worthy of your praise (Rev. 5:12).

Praise is your best weapon against Satan. When an alpha woman in Christ praises God, she is showing heavenly hosts, powers, principalities, demons of darkness, and angels of light that your great God is worthy of praise no matter what your circumstances. Praise produces victory, evokes praise. The process is recurring. Genuine praise must flow from your heart even during times of sorrow, discouragement, trial, and temptation (Ps. 42:5). The praise of His people brings glory to God. What a privilege it is to bring God joy!

Chapter 16
Beauty: More Than an Appealing Face

The Bible says a lot about inner beauty and outer beauty. Countless women in the Bible are well-known for their lovely appearance, such as Sarah, Rebekah, Abigail, Bathsheba, and Esther (Gen. 12:11; 24:16; 29:17; 1 Sam. 11:2; Esth. 2:7). Queen Esther had a beauty regimen (Esth. 2:3, 12). As a matter of fact, the account of a beauty pageant is found in the Book of Esther (Esth. 2).

An alpha woman in Christ appearance should be a complement to her inner spirit and never a hindrance to the kingdom of God. Beauty is more than an appealing face or the latest fashion. For a godly woman, good hygiene, healthy skin care, appropriate attire, and gracious manners are all expected to be a means of presenting an outward appearance that attracts others toward her life and ultimately gives opportunity for sharing a testimony of the Christ who dwells within her (2 Cor. 3:2, 3).

A woman's countenance is often a mirror of her heart. When she abides in God's love, her facial features tend to soften and lines become tempered. An inner peace and joy are reflected upon her face. A woman's actions and attitudes are often an indication of where her roots are planted. When a woman's heart is rooted in peace and joy (Gal. 5:22, 23), her outward countenance radiates vitality, enthusiasm, love, and a deep sense of well-being, something no amount of make-up, perfume, professional styling, high fashion, or personal fitness program can create. Having the Holy Spirit within empowers a woman with vitality and enthusiasm, making her a magnet to other people.

True beauty comes from within and is manifested by pure motives and a generous, unselfish spirit toward others. Jesus alone can establish such a wellspring of love (1 Chr. 16:29) when a woman yields her life to Him. No beautification regimen or stylish clothes can mask an unattractive heart, unkind words, or hurtful actions.

Chapter 17
Education: Studying with Him

The Lord is the alpha woman in Christ's ultimate Teacher (Ex. 4:15; Ps. 25:8; 9, 12); we are His students (Job 6:24). The first and foremost textbook is to be His commandments, the inspired account of the life of Jesus, and the divine revelation of the Holy Spirit (Prov. 6:23; Luke 12:12; John 14:26).

The curriculum includes:

- Fear of Lord (Ps. 34:11-14) His laws and the outworking of those laws;
- His truth (Ps. 86:11) the nature of the Lord and His promises to us;
- Right judgment (Is. 28:26) the ability to distinguish between good and evil, right and wrong;
- The to profit from His blessings (Is. 48:17-19) and to be in position to receive all His benefits, including peace, righteousness, and righteous children;
- The difference between what is holy and unholy (Ezek. 44:23, 24) how to discern what is of God;
- Wisdom (James 1:5) the way in which to live in good relationship with both God and man.

We as alpha woman in Christ are to be humble (Ps. 25:9), eager to learn (Prov. 12:1), and obedient (2 Tim. 3:14). We are to share generously our worldly goods with those who teach us God's Word (Gal. 6:6). We are to remember His lessons and diligently do what He has taught us to do (Deut. 4:9). Above all, we are to learn with our wills as well as with our minds. We are to live out, not simply know, His laws.

Chapter 18
Envy: Discontent with What You Have

Envy begins when contentment is interrupted by an awareness of the advantages enjoyed by another followed by the determination to seize such advantage whether in social standing, material possessions, or personal praise (Gen. 26:14; 30:1; Ps. 73:3). To want what others have has become a part of our culture of abundant things accompanied by the expectation that life should continually escalate to something better, easier, and more affluent.

Scripture says that envy co-exists with "every evil work" (James 3:16). Envy is commonly included in the New Testament vice list, and the list is ugly; striving, self-seeking, malice, deceit, hypocrisy, and evil speaking (Phil. 1:15; James 3:14-16; 1 Pet. 2:1-3). Envy is a disastrous emotion because it displaces our trust that God knows best and will supply our needs.

Even an alpha woman in Christ is capable of envying the good that others have received from God whether a leadership position, spiritual power, family relationships (especially children), or spiritual gifts. In so doing, she generally fails to reach her own potential in Christ Jesus. In seeking more that does not rightfully belong to her, she actually is diminished, a stated described in Scripture as "leanness of soul" and "rottenness of the bones" (Ps. 106:13-15; Prov. 14:30).

Alpha women in Christ escape envy only by giving our desires to God so that He might satisfy them in His timing and by His methods. When you do so, you find that the love of God transforms your emotions. Contentment with what you have and in whatever state you find yourself replaces envy (Phil. 4:11). You will receive a new long-range perspective of what is really important.

Chapter 19
Communication: Exchanging Ideas

Communication is the exchange of ideas and information by talk, gestures, or writing. It is an active process present in all meaningful relationships. Communications is not only talking but also listening, looking, and feeling. Though individuals have different communication styles, alpha women in Christ are to seek continually to improve their communication with other people and with God.

Speech is powerful. The spoken word can either encourage or discourage. Scripture teaches alpha woman in Christ to control the tongue (James 3:1-12) and speak only words of kindness (Eph. 4:29, 32). The Book of Proverbs discusses the importance of listening with understanding to others who speak (Prov. 11:12; 18:2, 13; 29:20).

Words alone cannot fully express meaning. Body language, facial expression, tone of voice, and other means of nonverbal communication are essentials for effectiveness. Obviously, communication is more than conveying information. Women especially use communication to express feelings more than facts, to establish rapport more than to give a report.

Paul underscores the significance of communication and gives advice about verbal behavior (Eph. 4:25-32).

Alpha women in Christ are to:

- Speak the truth in love
- Control angry words
- Speak words of encouragement and healing
- Avoid unkind or bitter speech
- Speak words of forgiveness

Alpha women in Christ realize that clear, loving communication is important in conveying the message of salvation effectively.

Chapter 20
Happiness: A Positive Choice

Happiness can be defined as a feeling of spiritual contentment that will carry you through the triumphs, pitfalls, or even heartaches of life with calm stability, serenity, peace of mind, and tranquility (Matt. 5:3-12). Happiness may or may or not be related to the happenings in your life. In most instances, the outward happenings in a life affects an alpha woman in Christ's attitude. But, happiness is also an act of the will (Ps. 144:15). Alpha women in Christ have things happening in our lives that give us reason to be unhappy, but we have the power through Christ to make our own response to those happenings. Happiness is a potential positive choice.

Jesus gives some characteristics that promote a response of happiness (meekness, righteousness, merciful, peacemakers; Matt. 5:3-11). An alpha woman in Christ must concentrate not on doing, but on being and living! Total commitment to the Lord will result in an alpha woman in Christ having instinctive Christ-like response to various happenings as they occur. She must appropriate the tools God has given (His Word and His indwelling Spirit) in order to pursue happiness (Prov. 3:1, 29:18). When an alpha woman's faith and conduct are balanced, happiness will always result. Happiness is enjoying everything the Lord has given you and not fretting about the things that have been taken away or withheld (Matt. 6:33, 34). Happiness is trusting in God's sovereignty and omniscience. An alpha woman in Christ must believe that every happening God will work for your good (Rom. 8:28). Happiness comes from daily obedience and faith in the Lord.

Chapter 21
Pain: Turning Physical Affliction into Joy

Pain was a part of the God-given consequence to mankind for believing Satan and disobeying God in the Garden of Eden. Women were to experience pain in childbirth and men, the pain of labor as they worked the ground (Gen. 3:16, 17). As a result, the "whole creation groaneth and travaileth in pain" (Rom. 8:22). Everyone is subject to pain until God brings "a new heaven and a new earth" and "there shall be no more pain" (Rev. 21:1, 4).

Job, "a perfect and an upright man" (Job 2:3), experienced pain as a result of Satan's direct attack. Job illustrates what often happens when a person experiences unrelieved pain. He isolated himself. His wife became impatient and lacked understanding. Job's focus was on himself, even on to the point of desiring death as a release (Job 3:20, 21).

The New Testament emphasizes pain's partnership with joy. The woman, through labor, experiences the joy of new life (John 16:21). Paul and Silas sang and prayed while in pain, and the result was their deliverance and the salvation of their jailer's household (Acts 16:23-25, 34). Perhaps Paul knew of the medicinal value of a "merry heart" (Prov. 17:22). Christ, who endured the Cross for the joy that was set before Him (Heb. 12:2), understands pain. He walks with Christians through their painful hours (Ps. 9:9, 10; Is. 41:10).

Chapter 22
Self-Esteem: A Healthy You

Self-esteem is how each alpha woman in Christ values herself. Poor self-esteem (bad, condemning, feelings about yourself) are weights that can keep an alpha woman in Christ under condemnation and cause them to be less than what God intends. Alpha women in Christ are to combat such feelings of inferiority (Heb. 12:1).

Proper self-esteem in an alpha woman in Christ is a matter of recognizing and confronting yourself in your humanity, including the tendency to sin, "going astray" (1 Pet. 2:25). It is also a matter of embracing Jesus' work on the Cross, His grace that covers a multitude of sins. The process of comprehending God's infinite care for the individual each with unique strengths and weaknesses puts a perspective on self-esteem. Psalm 139 express the wonder of being uniquely created by God and the intimate care of His presence at all times. Jesus tenderly described His love for His children (Matt. 6:25-34).

Prerequisites to healthy self-esteem include these:

- Recognize the need of a Savior (Is. 53:6).
- Accept being "in the beloved" (Eph. 1:6; Rom. 8:1).
- Move forward in God's plan for your life (Phil. 3:13, 14).
- Have a realistic view of yourself (Rom. 12:3).
- Avoid comparisons to others (2 Cor. 10:12).
- A person with healthy self-esteem is marked by these characteristics:
- Resting in ownership by God (1 Cor. 3:16).
- Submitting to being the "workmanship" of God (Eph. 2:10).
- Appreciating the differences of others (1 Cor. 12:1-31).
- Willingness to take risks, steps of faith (Esth. 4:13-16).

- Forging good relationships with others (Ruth 1:16, 17).

God does not evaluate human worth as we do. He looks to the heart within, while we tend to look only at the outer frame (1 Sam. 16:7; 1 Pet. 3:3, 4). The heart of a healthy self-esteem is recognizing that "self" must be seen as created for God's glory. Within every alpha woman in Christ there must be "God-esteem," which accepts whatever lot in life is ours.

Alpha women in Christ must be willing to change weaknesses into strengths when possible and when that is not possible, we are to look for opportunities for God to be glorified even in our failures and suffering. God does not make mistakes, and He is never finished working in us as He continues to refine and edify, helping each woman reach her maximum potential (1 Pet. 5:10). Negatives can be changed into positives and tragedies into triumphs with the Savior's touch.

Chapter 23
Healing of Shame: A Right Understanding of Self

Guilt is a God-given emotion that occurs when an alpha woman in Christ's mistakes and faults are brought to her own mind or publicly exposed. This may be a personal reminder of her own limitations and sinfulness. Shame, however, says that the person herself is bad, of no value, or unworthy to exist that she is hopelessly defective, unlovable, inferior, and worthless. Shame begins externally with a subtle implication through silence and neglect or with verbal denunciation through words of abuse. When such messages are repeated often enough, whether through words or actions, they become internalized into a false belief: I must be bad to deserve such terrible treatment. This becomes the core identity and the basis of thousands of future, flawed choices for the one suffering from shame.

Sometimes the victimizing acts done to a person may be so shame-producing that she is still emotionally bound by that shame, even though she mentally understands her worth in God's eyes. Or, if she herself has actually committed shameful acts, a deep sense of shame may remain even after confession and repentance. In these situations, those acts must be brought into the presence of Jesus. Ultimately, only He brings full emotional cleansing and freedom.

Chapter 24
Persecution: Hope Under Fire

The Bible records examples of persecution for the faith in both Old and New Testaments. Accounts of persecution in the Old Testament involved nations as a whole and individuals in particular. The prophets were persecuted because of their faith in God and their obedience to His will (Acts 7:52). In the New Testament, the church body, the twelve disciples, and individual Christians were persecuted for taking a stand for the Lord (Matt: 5:11, 12; 1 Cor. 15:9). Jesus suffered great persecution from the religious leaders of His day (John 5:16).

Persecution typically involves harassment and oppression for religious convictions, which results in physical or emotional suffering and affliction. Tribulation is to be an expected aspect of the alpha woman in Christ life, in part because Christians are to live according to standards and principles that are more righteous than those advocated by unbelievers (2 Tim. 3:12). However, persecution for the faith is neither unbearable nor useless (John 16:33).

Although persecution may be an inevitable part of a Christian woman's life, she is neither to seek out persecution nor bring persecution on herself. Much of what is perceived as persecution may actually be a consequence of abuse, a matter of poor self-esteem, or the result of an error in judgment. Alpha woman in Christ must be wise in discerning the true source of persecution and the motives that evoke it.

Persecution is also inevitable for these reasons:

- The sinful world hates God (John 15:18);
- The things of the flesh battle the things of the Spirit (Gal. 4:29);
- Tribulation is inevitable in the midst of righteous living (Matt. 5:10); yet

- Believers are undergirded with help, strength, and power from God to face their tribulations (Rom. 8:35-39).

Alpha women in Christ are to face persecution with patience, endurance, and steadfastness (Rom. 12:12; James 5:7-11). They are to endure persecution and, in the process, receive strength and power to be "more than conquerors" (Rom. 8:35-39). Blessing can actually be experienced in the midst of persecution (1 Pet. 3:14; 4:12-14) because the alpha woman in Christ facing persecution for the kingdom's sake is not forsaken by God (2 Cor. 4:7-10).

Chapter 25
Spiritual Warfare: The Armor of God

When a woman becomes a child of God, she not only inherits God's blessings but God's enemies as well. The Lord's foremost enemy is Satan, whose purpose is to destroy His work (John 8:44), but Jesus came in order to "destroy the works of the devil" (1 John 3:8). Satan is a fallen angel (Is. 14:12-15) and as such is only a created being. He is no way equal to God, the Creator. While Satan is superior in intellect and strength to mankind, he is inferior to God in every way. Alpha women in Christ have the power of the indwelling resurrected Christ over them and protection them (1 John 4:4).

Alpha women in Christ have been given the whole armor of God "to stand against the wiles of the devil" (Eph. 6:11). Each piece of the armor is to be put on to help alpha woman in Christ overcome the temptations and attacks of the Evil One.

1. Having Girded Your Waist with Truth: The waist or abdomen area was generally thought to be the seat of emotions. To gird this area with truth is to commit your emotions to believe the truth. Often a person knowingly allows herself to believe a lie because of fear or self-pity. Alpha women in Christ must hold a commitment to truth regardless of the repercussions (John 8:32, 36).

2. Having Put on the Breastplate of Righteousness (Eph. 6:14): The breast is generally thought of as the place of the soul. The heart must be kept pure and righteous because sin gives a foothold to the enemy. Confession and forgiveness on the basis of the blood of Christ cleans the heart (1 John 1:9).

3. Having Shod Your Feet with Preparation of the Gospel of Peace (Eph. 6:15): Proper shoes enable the feet to go from place to place. The alpha woman in Christ is to be about her Father's business, which is to

spread the gospel of peace and reconciliation. An undaunted sense of this mission keeps the woman headed in the right direction (Matt: 28:19, 20).

4. Taking the Shield of Faith (Eph. 6:16): The wicked one is "the accuser of our brethren" (Rev. 12:10) and will send his fiery darts to instill doubt, fear, and guilt. Faith acts as an invisible shield that deflects such false accusations (Heb. 11:6).

5. Take the Helmet of Salvation (Eph. 6:17): A helmet protects the head that is the brain and thoughts. Assurance of salvation is a mighty defense against doubt and insecurity and the kinds of works bred by them (1 John 5:11-13).

6. Take the Sword of the Spirit (Eph. 6:17): The Word of God, the only offensive weapon in this armor, was used by the Lord Jesus against Satan (Luke 4:1-13). The living Word is powerful, effective, and instructive (Heb. 4:12; 2 Tim. 3:16, 17).

7. Praying Always (Eph. 6:18): Prayer opens the channels between us and God. In the midst of battle we as alpha women in Christ must keep in constant communication with our Leader for directions and encouragement. Our prayers for one another are important and effectual (James 5:16).

Chapter 26
Stress Management: Peace That Passes Understanding

Through prayer, supplication, and thanksgiving, an alpha woman in Christ can realize a "peace…which passeth all understanding" and know that this peace "shall keep your hearts and minds" (Phil. 4:6, 7). Your natural human desire for acceptance, status, and possessions can create tension within. If you perceive that your needs or desires are not going to be meet, you may experience anxiety and stress. How can you "be careful for nothing" in the face of such situations?

Managing stress for an alpha woman in Christ begins with understanding yourself and knowing what Scripture teaches about the nature of God. To understand yourself means to know your basic nature, the potential of your strengths, and the limits of your weaknesses. This is no small task, for self-deception can prevent clear discernment (Jer. 17:9). Pride and independence can block self-awareness. God Himself must give the self-awareness needed (Jer. 17:10). Only He cans show clearly where change is needed and bring about that change in basic human nature (Ps. 139:23, 24).

An understanding of the nature of God comes from His self-revelation in Scripture and in Christ (John 1:14, 18). Knowing and accepting the unchanging nature of God produces stability and peace (Mal. 3:6; Heb. 13:8). Understanding the quality of His character inspires trust (1 John 1:5). Much of stress dissipates when you acknowledge your dependence upon God and submit to His leadership (Ps. 73:26; 1 Pet. 5:6, 7), recognizing that you are locked into time and space as finite creatures, while He is infinite, eternal, and omnipresent.

Chapter 27
Co-Dependency: A Quest to Meet Needs

The term co-dependency, with its diverse definitions, was coined in the context of treating alcoholism. But, it has evolved to mean a compulsion to rescue or control others by fixing their problems. Generally, co-dependency emanates from unmet or blocked God-given needs, such as love, acceptance, and security in primary relationships, as with parent, spouse, or child.

More frequently, co-dependency occurs in relationships with a dysfunctional person, resulting in a denial of the severity of the problem in the relationship, heightened sense of responsibility, and an environment of controlling or being controlled by others. It nearly always produces a keen sense of guilt or shame, hurt, anger, and loneliness in a complex and desperate quest to avoid abandonment. Ultimately, this need for acceptance can be filled by God alone. His unconditional love prepares the co-dependent to move toward complete healing.

Healing from co-dependency requires confession to God that something or someone has been put in His place. An alpha woman in Christ must then receive His forgiveness and grace (1 John 1:9, 10), establish effective and appropriate boundaries, and acquire new means of communicating and relating. Counseling may be appropriate and effective in finding complete healing (Prov. 11:14).

Chapter 28
Flexibility: Yielding Expectation

Flexible are the alpha women in Christ who yield themselves to the Lord and serve Him (Ex. 24:7; 2 Chr. 30:8), who submit to the Father's will even when it goes against what they personally desire to do (Matt. 26:42), and who choose to be obedient to Christ in their behavior and their thought lives (2 Cor. 10:4-6). The opposite of flexibility in Scripture is to have a "hard heart" and a "stiff neck" which includes resisting the Holy Spirit (Acts 7:51), being impudent and stubborn against the Lord (Ezek. 2:2-4), and worshiping false gods (Ex. 32:8, 9) all of which point toward a rebellious spirit. The person with a hard heart and stiff neck is subject to calamity and God's wrath (Prov. 28:14).

As an alpha woman in Christ in your relationships with others, you are to submit your will to those in authority (Heb. 13:17), "preferring one another" to others rather than demanding your own way (Rom. 12:10); yet, at the same time, abhor evil and stand up for what is good (Rom. 12:9). Above all, you are to be ready to present the good news of the gospel in any setting to everyone God sends to you.

Chapter 29
Time Management: Using God's Gift of Time

Time management is not just keeping busy but includes finding God's focus for you choosing a direction and moving ahead to accomplish your goals. Managing time is one of the most difficult yet helpful skills an alpha woman in Christ can develop. It takes maximum effort and realistic planning. First, an alpha woman in Christ must acknowledge that she has time the same amount God has given to everyone. An alpha woman in Christ with God's help must determine how to use her time (Prov. 3:5, 6). She errs in letting others decide her priorities and make her schedule (Rom. 12:2). Remember that by using small bits of time faithfully, an alpha woman in Christ can accomplish great things (Eccl. 9:10).

The foremost challenge an alpha woman in Christ faces is not to orchestrate her life or to plan her year but to order each day, allowing for sufficient rest, proper nourishment and exercise and exercise, and a quiet time spent exclusively with the Lord. To focus on what is really important, meaningful time must be assigned for vital relationships, especially with a spouse and children in the home.

The woman of strength arose early to plan for the day's activities (Prov. 31:15). Just as she had maidservants, women today have appliances, vehicles, as well as utility and telephone services. These blessing of God are ready to help and serve women in daily, mundane tasks, giving them a maximum amount of time to spend with the Lord and to serve others!

Chapter 30
Broken-Heartedness: A Shattered Life

The psalmist speaks of a "broken heart" and a "contrite spirit" (Ps. 34:18). A broken heart is experienced when someone else causes a breach in a relationship with us, while a contrite spirit results when we feel sorrow for having caused such a breach. Against either God or another human being. The alpha woman in Christ who experiences a broken heart, in many ways, is a victim in the wake of another person's actions, whether intentional or unintentional. The broken heart she experiences may be the result of abandonment, rejection, oppression, abuse, or even death. Regardless of the cause, the typical feeling is one of being devastated or feeling as if life has been shattered. Three other emotions are usually quick to arise: fear, loneliness, and despair. In many ways, a broken heart is a "broken spirit," in which you may lose the will to live, to love, or to trust.

One of the foremost roles of the Messiah, and one which Jesus embraced wholeheartedly (Luke 4:18), was to "bind up the brokenhearted" (Is. 61:1-3). Jesus very specifically addressed the underlying nature of a broken heart on several occasions. He dealt with fear (Mark 5:36), rejection and feelings of isolation (John 14:16), despair and loss of will (John 14:1).

The broken-hearted alpha woman in Christ finds healing when she chooses to believe again to believe that she will live, to believe that she will experience love again, to believe that God has a future purpose and plan for her life, or to believe that God will be with her always, even in the darkest hours of her hurt and sorrow (Jer. 29:11-14). In embracing fully the promise of Christ Jesus to heal her broken heart, she finds strength for reaching out to others, trusting that God still has something new for her (Lam. 3:22-27).

Chapter 31
Emotional Pain in the Depths of Despair

Lack of fulfillment in general and unfulfilled dreams in particular (Prov. 13:12) create emotional pain. Even in the presence of devoted love, sensitive areas in a person's life bring pain when "provoked." Emotional pain may exhibit itself in weeping, in altered appetite (1 Sam. 1:7), and in changed countenance (1 Sam. 1:18). This inward pain is described by the phrase "heart grieved" (1 Sam. 1:8), "bitterness of soul" (1 Sam. 1:10), and "grief" (1 Sam. 1:16).

Emotional pain is often misunderstood by others (1 Sam. 1:13, 14). Job's grief was harder to bear because his friends misunderstood him. This pain must be "poured out" to the Lord (1 Sam. 1:15), for Christ as "borne our griefs, and carried our sorrows" (Is. 53:4), and He does understand. The pain can be shared with someone He provides who is willing to listen and give support (1 Sam. 1:16, 17). That person needs to be a trusted person who has a "faithful spirit" (Prov. 11:13). God's children are to "bear ye one another's burdens" (Gal. 6:2). This support provides hope and lifts sadness (1 Sam. 1:18).

Chapter 32
Manipulation: Control vs. Trust

Manipulation is rooted in pride and selfishness, and involves viewing others as objects, not as individuals. It is an invasion of an individual's dignity because it seeks to limit freedom through control. The tools of manipulation are position, power, deception, and distortion. The results, even if perceived as successful, are always a denigration of God's best as the manipulative individual believes that she knows more than God.

Scripture has many vivid examples of manipulation of people and situations. Sarah manipulated her husband Abraham and her servant Hagar in order to influence what God had promised (Gen. 16:1-16). Rebekah manipulated her husband Isaac as well as her son Jacob in order to achieve her personal goal for her favorite son (Gen. 27:1-29). In these instances and countless others, manipulation brought more sorrow than joy (Gen. 16:5; 27:42, 43).

Anytime an alpha woman in Christ focuses on self rather than God, the possibility of manipulation exists. Fundamentally, such an attitude shows a lack of trust in God and suggests the erroneous belief that since God is not doing the right thing, we must take matters into our own hands and attempt to control environment, circumstances, and people by whatever means available. Manipulation is ultimately rooted in a lack of trust in God and a negative self-image that manifests itself in a driving need to control.

Chapter 33
Blended Family: Building a New Home

While the subject of blended families is not addressed specifically in Scripture, the Bible does give us alpha women in Christ some admonitions that seem relevant:

1. Build your new family on Christ. If mistakes were made in the past, seek the forgiveness of God, and others and turn away from the past in order to move with joyful purpose to future opportunities. Recognize openly that each family member has a distinct and irreplaceable relationship with Christ and that together you are mini-version of the body of Christ at work. Seek to understand and develop the unique spiritual gifts of each person in your family. Pray together. Make Christ the focal point and supreme authority of your home.

2. Clearly delineate the lines of authority and responsibility. The more responsibility a parent has for a child, the greater the authority he or she must have. Discuss openly and candidly with your spouse the need for defining clearly the roles of both parents over each child in your blended family in maintain order in the household (1 Cor. 14:40).

3. Foster communication. Heartfelt harmony, peace, and order require clear, direct, and convincing communication. Provide a regular forum for airing grievances, sharing ideas and opinions, and making family decisions, showing appreciation for each person's contribution (Eph. 4:29-32).

4. Recognize and value your differences even as you seek to blend together as a family. Allow each person the freedom to express his/her own personality, skills, and abilities within the constraints of family rules (Rom. 12:10-12).

5. Find and pursue mutually satisfying activities (Amos 3:3).

Chapter 34
Rape: The Ultimate Violation

An alpha woman in Christ who is raped may experience the same type of terror the Levite's concubine must have felt (Judg. 19:23-26). Physical death is not inevitable in every case of rape, but almost any victim does feel as though a part of her has died. A rape victim may suffer for some time from nightmares, severe and lingering fears, and feelings of low self-worth.

The victim of rape should be encouraged to recognize God's promise never to leave or forsake her (Is. 41:10; Heb. 13:5, 6). An alpha woman in Christ victimized by rape needs to seek comfort and healing from God, then from other believers (2 Cor. 1:3, 4). She must find a way of dealing with her anger toward her attacker. If she denies that anger, harbors it, or focuses on revenge, she is in danger of sinning herself (Heb. 12:14-16). On the other hand, as she forgives the one who has wronged her, she will open herself to recovery and growth (Matt. 6:14, 15).

The process of healing is not easy and takes time, but as a rape victim learns to rely on God for strength as well as healing, she will also learn that her experience may be used for the Lord's glory and honor, perhaps even by sharing the healing she has received from God with other victims.

Chapter 35

Miscarriage: An Experience of Bereavement

Through the experience of miscarriage is described in the Bible, the Hebrew word of miscarriage, translated as "cast their young," is seldom used in the Old Testament and never used in the New Testament. (Ex. 23:26; Hos. 9:14). Other forms can be translated "bereavement" in relationship to children. To be pregnant is to be "with child" (Ex. 21:22). To miscarry, an experience of bereavement, is to miss the opportunity to carry a child from conception until the child can live outside the womb.

As a child develops in the womb, an emotional bond between mother and child is established and grows in strength. The unborn child responds to things in the internal and external environment (Luke 1:41). The depth of grief following miscarriage varies according to the degree of bonding that has taken place between the parents and the child in the womb (Prov. 13:12). The miscarriage of a pregnant bystander (owing to a fight between men) carried a severe penalty (Ex. 21:22). The fine, proposed by the father and imposed by judges, may have been determined by the development of the child.

Hosea proposed "miscarrying wombs" as one of the consequences of Israel's longstanding, liberate disobedience to the covenant the Lord had made with Israel (Hos. 9:13-16). Miscarriage, however, was not viewed as judgment on selected women for personal sin. It is rather a consequence of living in a fallen world (Rom. 5:12, 14).

Both parents share in the loss of their child and need to be comforted by Christian friends (Eccl. 3:4; Rom. 12:15; Phil. 2:1, 2). The parents may need to be reminded that God's love encompasses the preborn and that He is involved in the development of the child in the womb (Ps. 139:13, 14). The "infants which never saw light" of day are at rest (Job 3:16, 17). Children, though lost to earthly life, are special to God (Mark 10:14), and Christian parents will one day be reunited with them (2 Sam. 12:23).

Chapter 36
Justice: Is God Fair?

Exodus repeatedly refers to the hardening of Pharaoh's heart. Clearly the purpose for this is not to present the Lord as capricious or unfair. To the contrary, the Lord is explicitly declared to be merciful (Ex. 33:19; 34:6, 7). The hardening of Pharaoh's heart is explained as an opportunity for the Lord to act in such a way that people then and now would know Him (Ex. 10:1, 2). He would receive due honor as a result of the hardening (Ex. 14:4, 17, 18). The Lord's care for His people (Ex. 6:6, 7; 8:22, 23), His uniqueness (Ex. 8:10; 9:14), and His sovereign ownership of the earth (Ex. 8:22; 9:29) are displayed by the plagues as part of the deliverance of the Israelites for Egypt.

Nothing in Pharaoh's speeches or conduct or in Egyptian history indicates that Pharaoh would have become a loyal worshiper of the Lord if the Lord had not hardened his heart. Apart from the hardening, Pharaoh might well have dismissed the Israelites simply in order to avoid difficulties and then continued his proud idolatry. The plagues and hardening demonstrate that Pharaoh and Egypt as a whole owed their existence to the mercy of the Lord, not to their cleverness in manipulating Him as they did the deities they worshiped (Ex. 9:15-17).

Because Pharaoh himself was considered an important god in Egypt, his ultimate personal destiny is not the primary issue in the hardening of his heart. His hardening contributes to the attack on the Egyptian religion and on pagan worship in general (Ex. 12:12; 18:11; 20:3-5; 34:10-17). For example, one Hebrew word describing the hardening of Pharaoh's heart has the connotation of making the heart "hardened" (Ex. 9:34; 10:1). This would be a major disadvantage within Egyptian religion, in which a person needed a light heart (rather than a sinful one) after death to weight favorably on the god's balance scale. In Egyptian thought, to be hard of heart was a positive trait. The idiom was used of strength and of self-restraint shown while serving at court. A person also needed a hard heart during judgment after death. To ensure that a person's heart would declare the person innocent rather than confess sins to the gods, a heart-shaped scarab made of a precious stone was placed on the chest of the mummified body. In Exodus, however, to have a hard heart is a negative trait, and when the Lord God hardened Pharaoh's heart, his sinfulness was displayed. Lofty Pharaoh appeared at a loss by Egypt's inadequate standards as well as in light of the Lord's righteous standards.

In answer to the questions asked by many; If God hardens the heart, why does He still find fault, for who has resisted His will? The Apostle Paul flatly asserted that God is not unjust (Rom. 9:14-24). In the process of Pharaoh's hardening, God showed patience toward those who deserved punishment, and He used the situation to make known His righteous wrath, saving power, and brilliant glory.

Chapter 37
The Lord's Day: A Time for Rest and Worship

The Sabbath which means "rest" is the seventh day of the Hebrew week (Gen. 2:2, 3). The Israelites were commanded to keep this day as a holy day of rest, reflection, and recreation in honor of the Lord (Ex. 20:8-11). The Sabbath served to remind the Israelites of their identity as God's covenant people and of their deliverance from Egypt (Ex. 31:12-17; Deut. 5:15; Is. 58:13, 14). It was a day that offered refreshment from work, both spiritually and physically (Ex. 23:10-12). Traditionally, Jews spend three days each week in eager anticipation of the Sabbath then after it has passed, three days reflecting on its joy. The Old Testament has very sharp reminders to keep the Sabbath day (Is. 56:2; Jer. 17:19-27; Ezek. 44:24), as well as harsh punishment for a person who broke the Sabbath (Num. 15:32-36).

The Lord's Day, by comparison, was considered to be the "first day" of the week. A sign of the new beginning marked by the Resurrection of Jesus from the tomb, the Lord's Day quickly became the day on which the early church met for weekly worship (Acts 20:7; 1 Cor. 16:2). Yet rest remains an important part of the Lord's Day. The Lord's Day is not to be filled with legalism, for that is what Christ frequently rebuked in His day. It should be the joyful focal point of the week, a day eagerly anticipated by the alpha woman in Christ. She should approach it physically rested and attitudinally ready for the Lord to reveal Himself to us (Ps. 118:24).

Chapter 38
God: He Is Personal

God is the Ultimate Being. He is living, speaking, loving, feeling, and seeking God. Though He is spirit (John 4:24), He has intellect (1 Cor. 2:10, 11), will (Dan. 4:35), and emotions (Deut. 4:21, 24), and He communicates with alpha women in Christ (Job 22:21, 22; Prov. 2:6). One of the pervading themes in Scripture is God's desire for a personal relationship with the man and alpha woman in Christ whom He created in His image.

God has used nearly every relationship of personal commitment we know to reveal Himself to us: husband (Jer. 31:32), father (Gal. 4:6, 7), mother (Is. 49:15), brother (Prov. 18:24), lover (Song), bride-groom (Rev. 19:7-9), shepherd (Ps. 23), creator and designer (Ps. 139:13-16), king (Ps: 10:16), provider (Matt. 6:25-33), protector (Jer. 20:11), teacher (Ps. 25:8-12), counselor (Is. 9:6), friend (John 15:14, 15), physician (Matt. 9:12, 13), master (Luke 16:13), servant (Mark 10:45), and military commander (Eph. 6:11-18).

The ultimate communication of God to us is Jesus (John 1:18; 10:30; 12:45; 14:9). Only the God of the Bible is the living God. He was not made by human hands (Is. 45:5-7; Col. 1:15-17; Rev. 1:8), but He made and fashioned the world and all that is in it (Ps. 100:3; 115:15; Eccl. 3:11). His greatest glory is found in His creation with whom He is personally and intimately involved and of whom Christ is the crowning expression.

Chapter 39
Clean and Unclean: A Divine Distinction

The biblical distinction between "clean" and "unclean" has nothing to do with hygiene. Rather, it is the way God designated the difference between what He could receive into His presence and what must remain apart from Him. Only people, animals, and objects designated as clean could enter the tabernacle, and later the temple, as part of the worship of God. Specific rituals were instituted by God for making an "unclean" person or object "clean" (Lev. 14; Is. 1:16).

The designation of "clean" and "unclean" also implies a distinction between ethical character and behavior that is acceptable to God ("holy") from that which is unacceptable ("unholy"). Jesus clearly taught that it is a person's character ("heart") which determines whether or not she is "clean" and can be received into God's presence (Mark 7:15). Because of the spiritual nature of human character, external rituals cannot make anyone admissible to the Lord's presence. Only the blood of Jesus Christ can make us "clean" and only through Him are we welcomed into the presence. Only the blood of Jesus Christ can make us "clean" and only through Him are we welcomed into the presence of God the Father (1 John 1:9).

Chapter 40
Holiness: Set Apart unto the Lord

Holiness describes the character of God and the code for Christian conduct. Scripture reveals the holiness of God and expresses God's desire for His children to develop a similar holiness (Ex. 19:6; Lev. 11:44, 45; 19:2; 1 Pet. 1:15). The word "holiness" has several different meanings. In terms of an individual's relationship to God, it means "set apart." God is the "wholly other" or totally different One, unlike any other. Holiness also describes a way to live. Christians are called to live according to a different set of principles and standards than the ungodly world to lead a pure life in accordance with God's call, commandments, and consequences. This "set apart" life of righteousness is of God and from God desires.

Obedient alpha women in Christ are instructed no longer to be conformed to their old desires and patterns of thinking and behaving (1 Pet. 1:13-16). The conforming to a life of holiness, however, requires more than the will of a person to "change." It is the work of the Holy Spirit made possible through Christ's death on the Cross.

True holiness is exemplified only in God, though the Holy Spirit empowers His children to pursue holiness (1 Thess. 4:7, 8). The good news is that as we seek to be holy and invite the Holy Spirit to do His work in us, the Lord responds by cleansing us, leading us into His righteous and holy paths, and strengthening us to withstand the temptation to return to our former ungodly lives. Alpha women in Christ cannot make ourselves holy, but if we desire to become holy and set our wills toward following the Lord, He will make us so. The Lord never commands us to do something that He does not enable us to do (Rom. 4:21).

Chapter 41
The Pastor's Wife: The Shepherdess

Shepherding God's people is a role that varies widely according to time and place, but biblical principles regarding leadership remain constant. In the Bible, "priest," "prophet," and "deacons" may refer to similar leadership positions, and many were unmarried because of difficult conditions and circumstances. Alpha women who married these men were inevitably linked to a twofold requirement: a life denouncing worldly gain and behavior modeling the highest spiritual standards of integrity.

Often testing is required to develop total faith in God for everyday sustenance. Elisha's advice to the newly widowed wife of one prophet illustrates the faithful provision of the Lord for His servants (2 Kin. 4:1-7). Paul taught that the laborer is worthy of his hire (1 Tim. 5:18), but God's people frequently failed or were too poor to furnish sufficient upkeep. The Mosaic Law assigned Aaron, the High Priest of Israel, and his tribe of Levi the oversight and care of all aspects of corporate worship. The Levitical priests were to represent God to the people until the Law was fulfilled in Christ. This demanded a life of holiness. Their wives were hand-picked virgins (Lev. 21:7, 13). The Law from Sinai adequately provided for support of the priest and their families (Num. 18:8-20), but in later years poverty and spiritual defection were recorded. Malachi strongly denounced divorce and personal decay in the priesthood (Mal. 2:11). In writing to Timothy, his young pastor protégé, Paul, delineated qualities of reverence and self-control needed in the wives of spiritual leaders (1 Tim. 3:11, 12). Modern church life still calls for women with a high level of commitment to serve as wives of pastors. To balance marriage, home, and family with exemplary devotion and dedication to the ministry requires unselfish teamwork and zealous compassion for the cause of Christ.

Chapter 42
The Sanctity of Life Created in His Image

God places special value on human life (Gen. 1:26; Ps. 8:4-6). Human life is sacred because the man and woman alone were created in the image of God, and that life deserves protection. God commands His people to protect and defend innocent human life (Ezek. 16:20, 21, 36, 38). Under the Mosiac Law, the murder of another person deserved punishment by death because of the value of the life that was destroyed (Gen. 9:6; Ex. 20:13).

Scripture extends this special status and protection to human life in every stage of development and need (Is. 46:3, 4). The unborn child shares in God's image (Ps. 139:13-16) and is protected under Old Testament law (Ex. 21:22-25). Believers are exhorted to defend and care for the sick, the elderly, and the poor (Lev. 19:32; Deut. 15:7, 8). No one is excluded from protection and care. Throughout history, this biblical view of the sanctity of all human life has faced opposition most notably from those who advocate a "quality of life" viewpoint, suggesting that human life must possess certain qualities and abilities before it can be considered truly valuable and worthy of life sustenance. According to this distorted humanistic view, if the unborn child, the handicapped infant, or the elderly person does not possess these qualities that individual is not entitled to the protection which Scripture or the Law would give.

The Bible rejects this "quality of life" view. The value of human life does not depend upon the person's functional abilities or independent viability but is assured because of the image of God that is found in every human life. God does not measure the quality of a human being before He bestows His image. God calls upon us to extend our care and compassion to every life He has created, in every stage of development and in every need.

Chapter 43
Debt: A Form of Bondage

From a biblical perspective, debt puts a person into a form of bondage; the indebted person is a "servant" to the lender (Prov. 22:7). One of the most significant problems with debt is that it always presumes upon the future (Job 8:9). When a woman chooses to borrow, she presumes that she will have means available to repay her debt in an uncertain and unknown future. James 4:13-16 warns against the assumption that you will be able to control future events. The point is that the future is in God's hands (Acts 1:7).

To borrow without repaying is not an option for an alpha woman in Christ (Ps. 37:21). Two of Jesus' parables deal with the matter of repaying money that has been loaned (Luke 16:1-8; 19:12-27). Believers were instructed that borrowed items were always to be returned (Ex. 22:7-15; 2 Kin. 6:5). Lenders are admonished to be generous in loaning to the poor (Ps. 37:26). The law provided for the poor who were unable to repay a debt to have that debt cancelled every seventh year (Deut. 15:7-11), a reminder that God is bigger than all problems, including financial ones. Going into debt may deny God the opportunity to work (Is. 55:8, 9). He can work in exciting ways if we trust Him to do so.

Chapter 44
Suffering the Dilemma of Helplessness

Perhaps the most brutal and degrading form of suffering is violent ill-treatment. The subject of rape appears in the story of King David's daughter, Tamar (2 Sam. 13:1-22). The subject of death is met in the account of Jephthah's daughter (Judg. 11:29-40). Jephthah, quite apart from God's will, makes a vow that if he were to win in battle, he would offer as a burnt offering the first person to greet him on his return home. His only daughter became this person, and to save face, he carried out his vow. The tragic irony for Jephthah was the fact that God wished to give him the victory without any such deal. In the end, his daughter gained the true victory because in her obedience to her father, her name was perpetuated among the women of Israel in a way in which neither her father nor any subsequent offspring could ever have ensured.

The Bible does not present an easy solution to the problem of suffering. Rather, the suffering of Christ is our model. By participating in our suffering through His own suffering and by rising from its absolute destruction, Jesus Christ has shown us that beyond the awfulness of human suffering is a way to victory that serves somehow to transform our fallen world to its former glory (2 Tim. 3:12; Heb. 5:8).

Chapter 45
Fear: Shutting God Out

The admonition to "fear not" is frequently repeated in Scripture. Fear is described as bondage (Rom. 8:15), torment (1 John 4:18), and a snare (Prov. 29:25). Often the phrase "neither be dismayed" (torn apart panicked) accompanies the command to "fear not." Scripture offers a long of things about which believers are not to worry: provision (Matt. 6:25), enemies (Deut. 1:21), other gods (2 Kin. 17:35), death (Ps. 23:4), armies and wars (Ps. 27:3), reputation (Ps. 71:24), evil days (Ps. 49:5), children (Ps. 127:3), the future (Ps. 139:1-6), sudden terror (Prov. 3:25, 26), safety (Matt. 10:28), events beyond your control (Matt. 8:26), health (2 Cor. 12:7-10), fearful thoughts (Phil. 4:6, 7), words of others (1 Pet. 3:14), and suffering (Rev. 2:10).

Reasons are also given for not fearing: You are His creation (Is. 44:2); He fights for you (Ex. 14:13); you are loved (1 John 4:9); He is your helper (Heb. 13:6); you are not more valuable than the sparrows (Luke 12:7). The reason given most often is God's presence (Gen. 26:24; Deut. 31:8; Rom. 8:15). You do not need to ask for God's presence, He is with you; you have His word on it. But you often need to ask for an awareness of His presence (Is. 41:10, 13). This awareness is most often prompted by remembering His faithfulness in the past (Deut. 7:18, 19).

Chapter 46
Contentment: The Ultimate Acceptance

Contentment is the ultimate acceptance of yourself, your surroundings, your past, and your future. For an alpha woman in Christ, finding contentment should be effortless. Jesus has paid the price for your sin and has given you a secure future of eternity in His presence, free of all pain and sorrow (Eph. 2:8, 9; Rev. 21:4). The suffering you experience now should be viewed in light of an eternity to be spent with the Savior (Rev. 21:7). God provided a way for you to be rescued from an eternity in hell. He is sufficient to meet your needs in this world that He created (Phil. 4:13, 19).

Yet reaching this blessed state of contentment is not an easy task. Satisfaction when you have very real unmet needs, freedom from worry when you have overwhelming concerns, patience in letting God work when pressures abound, these seem like impossible dreams. Happiness despite heartaches caused by the past, in the midst of tragedies experienced in the present, based on promises trusted of the future, is not merely a human pursuit but demands spiritual resources only found in the indwelling Holy Spirit.

God chose not to give you contentment as a gift. He chose rather to teach you to be content as you allow Him to be ruler in your life. Contentment is learned (Phil. 4:11). As you trust God's gifts to be sufficient and His assignments to be appropriate, you can accept the way you look, the means you have been given, the family in which you are living, the struggles through which you have gone, the job you have, being content and fulfilled in all (2 Cor. 3:5, 6; 12:9).

On the other hand, acceptance does not mean stagnation. Dissatisfaction with areas in your life that can be changed, within divine guidelines, may help you to see that something is missing. When this happens, you dare not adopt the "Canaan syndrome" of complaining. Remember that God's people were not allowed to enter the Promised Land because of their murmuring (Josh. 5:6).

Rather, take that dissatisfaction to the Lord and see what He would challenge you to do, being willing in the meantime to be "content" as you work toward ultimate goals. This is the balance between "I have learned to content," and "I can do all things through Christ" (Phil. 4:11, 13). You must trust that God has given you everything needed for this moment in time. You should be content with yourself, your family, your surroundings, your job, or your past. As you depend on the Lord, you are content as you pursue His goals for your life.

Chapter 47
Wealth: Blessing or Curse?

The Bible teaches that wealth comes from God and will be returned to Him. Wealth should bring praise to God. At times, God chooses to bless His children alpha women in Christ with wealth. Abraham, Isaac, Solomon, and even Job received wealth as a blessing from God (Gen. 13:2; 26:12-14; 1 Kin. 3:13; Job 42:12). Material wealth is given to mankind as a stewardship. God, the owner of all things, expects His children alpha women in Christ to care for His possessions and return them to Him (Luke 12:42). Wealth is also intended to bring praise to God. Believers who give money to help others bless the Lord (2 Cor. 8:1-5).

Sixteen of the thirty-nine parables of Jesus deal with wealth. In Scripture, more references are made to money than salvation. Jesus dealt with money because money matters to people. Material wealth can be a blessing or a curse. The power of wealth is subtle (1 Tim. 6:10). The source of wealth is secure (Matt. 6:25, 26). The temptation of wealth is spending (James 4:3). The strategy of wealth is saving (Matt. 25:27). The purpose of wealth is sharing (Acts 20:35).

God expects His children to use the wealth they receive from Him to bless others and to bring glory to Him. In the parable of the talents, Jesus promised an abundance to all who possess His kingdom and eternal life to all who trust in Him (Matt. 25:14-30).

Chapter 48
Dating: Relating to One Another

Dating relationships are not described in Scripture. You can assume, however, that dating is subject to God's general principles pertaining to relationships. God is very clear about how you are to relate to one another.

1. Dating teens must honor their parents and respect their counsel (Eph. 6:2).
2. The dating partner must be considered. God's Word is very clear when it says, "Be ye not unequally yoked together with unbelievers" (2 Cor. 6:14). You are wise to ask whether or not your date has a personal and growing relationship with the Lord. Also, you should consider whether that relationship is evident in your date's lifestyle.
3. You must examine yourself. Are you spending time with the Lord daily (Matt. 6:33)? Are you depending on the Lord to meet your needs of love and security? Are you an example for Christ to all those with whom you have contact (1 Tim 4:12)? The Lord calls for you to have a loving relationship with and a commitment to Him that supersedes any dating relationship.

Chapter 49
Women's Ministries: Teaching God's Word

Teaching is a gift (1 Cor. 12:28, 29; Eph. 4:11; Rom. 12:7) that God's Spirit gives to both women and men. All alpha women in Christ are to teach one another (Col. 3:16) and to share with the community what they have learned (1 Cor. 14:26). Priscilla, together with her husband Aquila, instructed a Christian brother, Apollos, in matters of theology (Acts 18:26). The apostle Paul recognized Priscilla's ministry and obviously loved and respected her as well as other female co-laborers (Rom. 16:3, 6, 12; Phil. 4:3). Paul also encouraged older women to teach the younger women (Titus 2:3-5) and admonished Timothy to respect Lois and Eunice, his mother and grandmother, for instructing him in the faith (2 Tim 1:3-5). Although Paul was a great advocate for women to exercise spiritual gifts, he taught that gifts needed to be exercised in a manner that honors the Word of God (1 Tim. 2:12). New Testament women were encouraged to exercise teaching ministries but were to do so within the God-ordained pattern of male-female complementarity.

Chapter 50
Goodness

God's goodness is expressed in creation (Gen. 1:31) and experienced in salvation (Phil 1:6). The psalmist proclaims the goodness of God as great (Ps. 31:19) and as eternal (Ps. 23:6; 52:1). God is the true essence of goodness, the Author of unlimited, undeserved generosity. Though God alone is truly good, Scripture encourages believers to seek goodness by modeling their lives after Christ Jesus. For the alpha woman in Christ, goodness is not simply the absence of evil; it is righteousness accompanied by acts of kindness. As a fruit of the Holy Spirit, goodness is a natural result of love, joy, peace, long-suffering, and kindness at work in a person's life (Gal. 5:22, 23). It is the outward expression of inward change in an alpha woman in Christ's heart the invisible power of a Holy God overcoming the sinful nature that is in all people.

True goodness is difficult to attain. It manifests itself only in a life totally committed to the Lord and is a requirement for effective ministry. Service to others is counted as evidence of the goodness of God at work in the life of a believer (2 Thess. 1:11, 12).

Chapter 51
Identity in Christ: A Member of His Family

Alpha women in Christ are secured by the supernatural glue of the Trinity. To be separated from Christ would require prying open the hand of the Father (John 10:29) and being snatched from the Son after breaking the seal of the Holy Spirit (Eph. 1:13, 14). Jesus became one of us so that we could be one of His family (Eph. 2:19). Just as a newborn baby girl arrives with a genetic code (2 Cor. 5:17, 18), in accepting Christ and bonding ourselves to Him through faith, each one of us becomes a new creation with forgiveness for sins in the past, guidance and nurture for the present, and security and hope in the future (2 Cor. 5:17).

Alpha women in Christ have access to all that Jesus is; we, as joint heirs, potentially have all He has (Rom. 8:17). God hears us because He hears Christ (Heb. 4:14-16) and loves us the way He loves Christ (Rom. 8:39). In a nutshell, identity in Christ means every child of God can point to Jesus and before the Father's throne testify: "I'm with Him."

Chapter 52
Giving: A Generous Heart

A generous heart is one marked by evidence of the Holy Spirit's work in your life. God's love is demonstrated in the giving of His Son (John 3:16). Giving time, energies, and financial resources is the expression of a grateful heart, the natural response of an alpha woman in Christ who realizes she has been lavished with God's grace (Eph. 1:7, 8).

In the Old Testament, the Jewish tithe (the first one tenth) was a prescribed percentage of a person's income. It belonged to the Lord and was used to provide for the priests, the temple, and the needy. Offerings were made on special occasions (Ex. 35:21; 36:7) and as an obligatory part of public sacrifices of thanksgiving, blessing, or sorrow.

In the New Testament, emphasis is placed upon the alpha woman in Christ's heart and attitude. Paul declared that a Christian's giving should be the overflow of a worshipful heart and a matter of conviction before God (2 Cor. 9:7). Giving to others in a spirit of forgiveness without judgment or condemnation brings joyful, abundant rewards (Luke 6:37, 38).

Chapter 53
Guilt: A Spiritual Weight

Guilt is the emotional and spiritual weight we bear as the result of sin against others and against God. Christ taught that the acknowledgement of our true guilt is the door through which we can experience the cleansing and renewal of being forgiven (1 John 1:9, 10). There are two kinds of guilt: false guilt and true guilt. False guilt is what the apostle Paul refers to as "the sorrow of the world" (2 Cor. 7:9, 10). He describes a nebulous sense of free-floating regret and guilt which seem to have no clear source and leave only a deep feeling of condemnation. True guilt, on the other hand, is "godly sorrow that worketh repentance to salvation."

True guilt is the gentle, persistent prodding of the Holy Spirit, which leads an alpha woman in Christ to acknowledge that she has indeed failed or fallen short of God's law (Rom. 3:23). That recognition of failure compels us to repent and seek God's forgiveness and to experience once again the freedom and restoration made possible by Christ's all-sufficient sacrifice (Rom. 5:10). Guilt that leads to repentance liberates the soul.

Chapter 54
Appearance: Unfading Beauty

Alpha woman in Christ should be a complement to the kingdom of God in every aspect of life (2 Cor. 3:2, 3). Maintaining a clean, neat, modest, and appropriate appearance is a responsibility. To neglect how you look can diminish your total effectiveness since Scripture describes your body as the dwelling place of the Holy Spirit (1 Cor. 3:16, 17; 6:19, 20)! What's nurtured internally is ultimately manifested externally (Prov. 23:7).

Appropriate attire is essential for women who represent Christ. Women are admonished not merely to have outward adornment but to use such adornment to emphasize what is within (1 Pet. 3:3, 4). A Christ-like spirit is preferred over excessive make-up, gaudy jewelry, or revealing clothes. Style and beauty, however, need not be compromised. Alpha women in Christ can be stylish with modesty and flair! Good manners also blend into your total image. Consideration of another's feelings and opinions is an opportunity to reflect the character traits described in Scripture as the fruit of the Spirit (Gal. 5:22, 23). Having appropriate social skills can relax and free you to impart energy and concentration in other areas, such as sharing a witness for Christ or extending hospitality. Christians are watched, and their lives are scrutinized (Matt. 5:16). How others interpret your words and actions will be, to a great extent, how they regard Christ's love ought to shine! Unfading beauty is not dependent upon the outer frame but is achieved with the balance of personifying Christ's love and taking care of God's handiwork (1 Pet. 3:3, 4).

Chapter 55
Humility: A Yielding of the Heart

While the Old Testament understanding of humility includes lowliness or affliction, its New Testament meaning is primarily a personal quality of dependence on God and respect for other people. Humility is not a natural human instinct; it is a God-given virtue of holy living.

The essence of the mind of Christ was humility at and sacrificial love for others, while the essence of the unregenerate human mind is selfishness and pride. Jesus Christ's life provides the perfect example of humility. Though He was and is eternal deity, Jesus appropriated humanity with all the attributes of that personhood except sinfulness (Phil. 2:5-8). Accordingly, believers should take heed to humble themselves to be what they need to be.

During a time when the Greek world abhorred the quality of humility, Christ came as a humble Savior. He humbled himself to become obedient to God's will, which led to His death on the Cross. Jesus urge alpha women in Christ to humble themselves before God and man (Matt. 23:12; Luke 14:11; 18:14) and to practice humility (Matt. 18:1).

Chapter 56
Creativity: Expressing Your Gifts

Human creativity differs from that of the Lord God in two ways: His is capable of creating out of nothing, and His creativity is unlimited (Gen. 1:1-2:3). Human creativity is locked into the natural world and is limited to that which can be experienced and thought, and in many respects, to that which can be articulated or framed in language, art, or music.

Because humans are created in the image of a creative God, they have the potential for creativity, which may surface in a myriad of ways: resolving a problem, hatching an idea, adapting a recipe, stretching a budget, or many other expressions of self. Creativity is not limited to the artistic but adds to all of life a personal imprimatur with zest and joy. Creativity is not necessarily originality but rather a determination to bring about change (2 Cor. 5:17). This ultimately means losing both self and limitations in Christ.

Creativity demands focus, commitment, and discipline. Alpha women in Christ are to create only that which is for good (1 Pet. 4:19), and they must never worship that which was created (Rom. 1:25). They must look within for God-given gifts, believe in divinely appointed abilities, maximize circumstances and situations, wait with patience for guidance from the Holy Spirit, and proceed with perseverance to accomplish the tasks God has given. Failure is a useful tool for creativity because it may become a stepping-stone to something better. Sometimes creativity calls forth a new course of action (Phil. 3:12-14); always it presupposes a heart turned toward God (2 Cor. 5:17).

Chapter 57
Weight Control: A Disciplined Body

If an alpha woman in Christ struggles with weight control, God's Word has both encouragement and admonishment:

1. Be accepting. God designed your physical make-up. Refrain from criticizing His creation (Ps. 139:13-16).
2. Be grateful. God has given you a triumphal new nature at your conversion. You are admonished to give thanks to God who gives you victory in the Lord Jesus Christ (1 Cor. 15:57).
3. Be careful. The Bible, speaking for moderation and against gluttony, condemns over-indulgence (Prov. 23:20-21). Resist extra helpings and rich foods that add additional inches.
4. Be disciplined. Achieving temperance in eating will strengthen other areas in your life. Paul proclaimed that also that although all things were lawful for him, he refused to be brought under the power of any (1 Cor. 10:23) because all things were not helpful to him (1 Cor. 6:12).
5. Be active. Regular exercise will help you to reach and maintain your ideal weight. Activity also improves productivity, cardiovascular stamina, and mental alertness. The writer of Hebrews encourages believers to run with endurance (Heb. 12:1; 1 Tim. 4:8).
6. Be persistent. Just as Paul finished the race (2 Tim. 4:7), you, too, can persevere if you set a goal and move forward victoriously to achieve it!

Chapter 58
Mental Health: A Sound Mind

When Jesus referred to the abundant life, He described a life in balance, all aspects of which are under the authority of God, and one in which an individual would grow in the image of Christ. Elements necessary for positive mental health include: reasonable independence (Prov. 31:12-16), trustworthiness, the ability to take responsibility, the ability to show friendliness and love (Prov. 17:17), a sense of humor, the capacity to give and take (Eccl. 3:5), and most of all a devotion beyond self (1 John 4:10, 11). Jesus not only provided salvation but also underscored the quality of life and set new standards for the abundant life.

Because a healthy life is intertwined with a healthy mind, alpha women in Christ are warned by Paul to guard what the mind absorbs so that they do not become blinded to the truth (2 Cor. 3:14; 4:3, 4). Scripture strongly states that what goes into the mind comes out in actions, good or negative (Prov. 23:7; Mark 7:20-23). In healing the Gadarene demoniac, Jesus put him in his right mind (Luke 8:35). The restored man surely returned to a useful role in his home and community, and he did not forget to testify of God's goodness to him (Luke 8:39). Paul encouraged Timothy by saying, "For God hath not given us the spirit of fear; but of power and of love, and of a sound mind" (2 Tim. 1:7). Alpha women in Christ can certain the Lord wants us to enjoy excellent mental health.

Chapter 59
Worry: The Paralysis of Faith

Depending on context, words translated as "cares" and "concerns" or "fear" and "anxiety" can be either right or wrong attitudes in an alpha woman in Christ's life. Fear is right when it is reverence toward God because of His holiness (Is. 8:13); and care is good when showing concern for others (1 Cor. 12:25; 2 Cor. 11:28).

But worry is always wrong, for it paralyzes active faith in your life. When you worry, you assume responsibility for things you were never intended to handle. Jesus repeatedly taught: "Take no thought" (to divide the mind), even about the basic essentials of life (Matt. 6:25-34). Worry divides your mind between useful and hurtful thinking. Worrying does not change anything (Matt. 6:27) except to draw your focus away from God and His faithfulness and righteousness to concerns about the things of life, such as possessions and material goods (Matt. 6:31). Worry is choking, harmful emotion that saps your energy and elevates human strength and ingenuity above God's strength and His purposeful plan.

Sources of worry includes change, lack of understanding, and lack of control over your life. Worry opens the door to worldliness, that is, preoccupation with the things of this life. Though the children of Israel had watched God split open the Red Sea to deliver them from Egypt, they could not believe He would provide water in the desert to meet their needs. Worry is the opposite of faith, suggesting that God cannot be trusted to take care of you or to provide what you need (Phil. 4:19). Worry causes fear to crowd out faith. Whereas, in the final reckoning, "the fearful" are listed alongside the "unbelieving" (Rev. 21:8).

Chapter 60
Obsessions: Invading the Mind

An obsession is an idea, usually charged with emotion that repetitively and insistently invades the consciousness even if unwelcome. When these ideas are manifested in behavior patterns, they are called compulsions.

Obsessions often indicate serious underlying difficulties. They are pervasive and become problematic when they interfere substantially with the ability to think rationally. Obsessions are usually short-lived and can be minimized or negated by diverting your attention. They usually occur in one of the following ways:

1. impulsive obsessions, ideas that lead to actions which are repetitive and can be destructive (the persecution of Christians by Saul of Tarsus, Acts 8:3; Gal. 1:13);
2. inhibiting obsessions, doubts about actions (the actions and reactions of King David in his lust for Bathsheba, 2 Sam. 11:1-17); or
3. intellectual obsessions, questions about the purpose of life or ultimate destiny (the thought-provoking encounter of the rich young ruler with Jesus, Matt. 19:16-22).

Ultimately, only the Lord Jesus can remove the anxieties and worries that accompany obsessive behavior. God has challenged alpha women in Christ to trust Him with their cares (1 Pet. 5:7). Being free of obsession is part of experiencing "the mind of Christ," which is available to all believers (1 Cor. 2:16).

Chapter 61
Adversity: A Mountain to Climb

Adversity is not God's ultimate desire for His creation; yet, there is a clear message that God uses adversity. He is in control over the most adverse of circumstances or reversing the situation that led to adversity. Rather, the Bible points to the conclusion that instead of taking us out of adversity God is much more interested in taking us through it, using the adversity to effect something good in our lives (Is. 43:2; Rom. 5:3-5; James 1:2-4).

Naomi and Ruth provide a great example of triumph over adversity. Women in Bible times had few independent or self-sufficient rights. As a result, most women depended upon the patronage of father, family, or husband. To lack such a protecting relationship was to invite adversity in many appearances. Naomi's family left Judah and went to Moab in search of food. There Naomi not only subsequently suffered the loss of her husband but later the loss of her two sons as well. Completely unprotected in a foreign land, she determined to return to her native city Bethlehem for safety.

Naomi's story is significant because of the faithfulness of her daughter-in-law Ruth, who could have chosen the protection of her homeland, Moab, but rather gave up her own rights. Ruth, who could have chosen the protection of her homeland, Moab, but rather gave up her own rights. Ruth did not choose the suffering of widowhood, but she did choose the vulnerability and possible suffering involved in following Naomi back to Judah, turning her back on the security and protection of her family in Moab (Ruth 1). Here God clearly emerges as the Protector of the unprotected who place their faith in Him. The womanly wisdom of Naomi foreshadows Jesus' character as revealed in the New Testament where He seeks those in need of being defended. Naomi was able to direct Ruth to Boaz, her kinsman redeemer, who, was Ruth's husband, became a guardian both for her and Naomi. In this story of faith were to be sown the seeds that would ultimately result in the birth not only of Israel's greatest king, David, but also of the Lord Jesus Christ Himself. This is one of the clearest examples of how God's ultimate purpose is worked out through human adversity.

On a completely different plane, Esther first experienced adversity in being an orphan. Yet God provided loving nurture for her through her cousin Mordecai. Her utter trust in the sovereign God helped her to place all her human resources in God's hands, and as a result the Jews, God's people, were ultimately preserved. Adversity is something from which the human condition naturally recoils, but the higher message of the Bible exhorts alpha women in Christ to embrace every circumstance God sends or allows, even to go as far as to "count it all joy" in the hope that God's ultimate purposes will be fulfilled (James 1:20).

Chapter 62
Authority: Who's in Charge?

God Himself is the ultimate authority and the source of all human authority. Alpha women in Christ are commanded to recognize God's authority behind human governing institution by being compliant and respectful citizens.

Even when human authority, corrupted by sin, is bent on evil purposes, God is working concurrently through that power to accomplish His perfect purposes. This paradox is never more strikingly revealed than when Jesus, standing before Pilate said, "Thou couldest have no power at all against me, except it were given thee from above" (John 19:11). The purpose of the human authorities that led to Jesus' Crucifixion were stained with evil. At the same time, God's good, gracious, and loving purpose of redemption was being accomplished through those human powers, even though they did not acknowledge Him as the source of their authority.

All power and authority is God's alone and He uses it always for the ultimate good of His children. Even when we do not see the beginning or ending of God's plan, Alpha women in Christ have to trust Him to be the Alpha and Omega, Beginning and Ending of all things, including the events of our individual lives (Rev. 22:13).

Chapter 63
Perfectionism: An Unreachable Goal

The compelling need to be more than what you are capable of ever becoming is the driving motivation behind perfectionism. It stems from deep insecurity, a gnawing fear that being the woman God made you to be is somehow not good enough. The longing for absolute perfection is rooted in the lost recollection of Paradise. Within every alpha woman in Christ is an internal barometer of how things ought to be, a deep yearning for the perfection that only heaven will bring. Something inside knows that no matter how good things are they should be better. One day they will be, but not now. Knowing how it could be while living with how it actually is often causes an unhealthy tension.

Understanding the innate desire for perfection can lead to a deeper anticipation and hope in eternity. It also helps release the demand that life in the present must satisfy all longings. At the same time, the Lord calls each believer to pursue wholeness and soundness of spirit concepts that are frequently described as "perfect" in the New Testament (Matt. 5:48). The foremost trait you are called to perfect in your life is the ability to love (1 John 4:17-19). Completion or perfection as human beings is not possible, therefore, as a result of your own striving. It is the manifestation of God's work in you (Heb. 13:20, 21).

Chapter 64
Childbirth: The Miracle of Birth

Although Scripture often uses childbirth and motherhood as a metaphor, the reality and importance of birth is also present. The womb is the natural incubator prepared by the Creator for the protection and growth of the child. If birth occurs prematurely (Ex. 21:22-25) the result could be tragic, such as the death of the mother (1 Sam. 4:19-22) or the death of the child (Ps. 58:8; Hos. 9:14).

Other allusions to the birth process in Scripture include personnel, such as the midwives (Gen. 35:17; Ex. 1:15); props, such as the birth stool (Ex. 1:16); procedures, such as the cutting of the navel cord that binds the child to the mother and the cleansing of the child (Ezek. 16:4); and penalties, such as the woman's ritual uncleanness for forty to eighty days after the birth (Lev. 12:1-8).

Pain contrasts with joy in the miracle of childbirth. The conception and birth of a child exemplify God's greatest creative masterpiece (Gen. 1:26-28). The bringing forth of young from the womb is an experience marked by extreme contrast. Most women who have borne a child will agree that carrying they child is very uncomfortable, and the birth of the baby is downright painful. But the indescribable joy of the new life created encourages every mother to rejoice. The pain is quickly forgotten, "for joy that a man is born into the world" (John 16:21).

Chapter 65
Childcare: Protecting our Children

In Bible times, children seemingly always had care within the context of family often a larger extended family. Children were rarely out of reach of familiar, loving arms and authoritative, life-shaping discipline. Seeking child care beyond the family circle necessitates that parents attempt to recreate the special nurturing a parents attempt to recreate the special nurturing a parent can best provide in the protection and peace of the family circle. To build self-confidence, trust, and contentment from afar can be a stressful challenge for all.

Nothing seems worse, in biblical terms, than for us to feel we have been left as orphans, isolated and alone. Jesus assured His disciples, when they began to fear the worst about their future with Him, "I will not leave you comfortless: I will come to you" (John 14:18). Something in the nature of divine love finds its fullest realization when intimacy, nearness, and availability are there for the taking.

The story of divine love in the Bible reveals a being there quality from beginning to end. Child care outside the home may be expedient for some families, but such a decision should always be bathed in prayer and carefully weighed. If alpha women in Christ, as parents, are God's representatives to our children in this world, we must make sure that a being there quality is built into all our dealings with our children and make our decisions about child car accordingly.

Chapter 66
Organization: Ordering Our Days

The concept of organization in Scripture relates far more to our relationships with people than to the handling of things. Organization allows an alpha woman in Christ to move through life with order and purpose. This discipline is not reserved only for organized people, for God delights in helping each woman to turn weakness into strength and to bring order from chaos (1 Cor. 14:40). He redeems our time as well as our souls (Col. 4:5).

Smooth communication, effective problem solving, and successful task management, and coordination of life's pursuits is just as necessary for meaningful interpersonal relationships as for juggling events and sorting activities. The Lord insisted, through the advice of Jethro, that Moses establish a multi-tiered judicial system, which effectively places "men of truth" as rulers of thousands, hundreds, fifties, and tens (Ex. 18:13-26). Jesus created order so that the hungry crowds could be fed by seating the people on the grass, allowing the disciples to move freely among them with bread and fish (Matt. 15:35). Jesus, in sending out His disciples, organized them in teams of two gave them well-ordered guidelines (Mark 6:7).

Decision making, assignment of space, accomplishment of tasks, and clear lines of communication are ordered with one goal in mind that our lives and environment might be so ordered as to give maximum freedom for achieving His goals. In organizing home or office, priority should be given to policies and structures that benefit and bless people. People always matter more to the Lord than rules, a principle readily evident in the ministry of Jesus, who frequently overstepped the boundaries set by the religious leaders of His day in order to bring truth, comfort, and healing to those in need.

Chapter 67
Problem-Solving: Seeking God's Solution

The first step in overcoming problems, whether they are physical, emotional, or spiritual, is to admit you are in need and desire a change. Jesus asked the man who had been lying by the Bethesda Pool for thirty-eight years a very important question: "Wilt thou be made whole?" (John 5:1-15). In other words, "Do you care enough about your problem to do something about it even if it requires on your part some action, effort, sacrifice, or even suffering?" In other words, "Do you care enough about your problem to do something about it even if it requires on your part some action, effort, sacrifice, or even suffering?"

As is typical of so many in need, this man answered the Lord with self-pity. When Jesus sees you in need of help and sends a willing person to help, do you play the martyr role? "There's no hope for me. Nobody loves me." The alpha woman in Christ who clings to this attitude is unlikely to experience healing.

Because Jesus is gracious and knows your deepest desires, He often cuts through your weeping and self-martyrdom and puts you to the test. "Get up," He says. "Take your problem and move on. Do not wait for other people to pity you. Get up." If an alpha woman in Christ is in need of a touch from the Lord, ask yourself if you are so eager to be changed that you are willing to do something about your situation. When you let God know you are obedient to His will and eager to do whatever it takes for you to be whole, He will send Jesus in the form of person, a verse from His Word, or a new thought in your mind. Act upon what God tells you to do. He made you, and He knows how to fix precisely what is broken within you.

Furthermore, when you feel God's power bring about positive changes in your life, do not let doubters convince you these changes are only coincidence. Walk firmly away as did the man with his mat under his arm and say simply "Jesus healed me."

Chapter 68
Decision-Making: Tough Choices

Every alpha woman in Christ faces decisions with immediate and long-term consequences. For the alpha woman in Christ, wise decisions can be made with the confidence that God directs her every step as she seek His will in prayer, Bible study, and listening to the Holy Spirit, the divine Counselor (John 14:26; 15:26). While Scripture offers precise guidance for many issues in our daily lives, the Bible appears silent on others.

In all cases, you can benefit from the principles Paul offered to the first-century Corinthian believers who were facing the moral dilemma of eating meat sacrificed to idols:

1. Will the course considered lead a fellow Christian to sin by your example? (1 Cor. 8:13)
2. Will the action provide strength and encouragement to your own life? (1 Cor. 6:12; 10:23)
3. Will the action ultimately glorify God? (1 Cor. 10:31)

These same questions are appropriate for your prayerful consideration in every decision you make.

Chapter 69
Celibacy: A Vow of Abstinence

To be celibate is to refrain from sexual intercourse. In Scripture, sexual behavior is always considered subject to the will. For a believer to live in purity is a personal obligation to obey fully the commandments of the Lord.

For some, celibacy becomes a lifelong vow so that they might more fully and completely give themselves to the Lord and His church (1 Cor. 7:32-34). It can be a call to love Christ whole-heartedly just as Christ loves the church (Eph. 5:29), to be "holy both in body and in spirit" (1 Cor. 7:34).

Celibate Christians have the opportunity to imitate Christ in a unique way during their earthly pilgrimage. Dying to self, they can focus their love on God for the sake of His kingdom (Matt. 19:12). For those who make such a commitment by faith, the Lord gives the grace to withstand sexual temptation and to live a sexually pure life (1 Cor. 7:17; 2 Cor. 12:9). The Bible does not advocate celibacy within marriage (1 Cor. 7:3-5), and Paul advises those who have strong sexual desires to marry rather than "to burn" with passion.

Chapter 70
Sexual Purity: Principle Must Rule Passion

The love life of an alpha woman in Christ is a crucial battleground. Each alpha woman in Christ must consider the authority of Christ over human passions, then set her heart on purity. Chastity means abstention from sexual activity outside of marriage and is a Christian obligation. For the alpha woman in Christ, there is one rule and one rule only: total abstention from sexual activity prior to marriage and total faithfulness within marriage (1 Cor. 7:1-9).

Alpha women in Christ are to prize the sanctity of sex. This means learning the disciplines of longing, loneliness, uncertainty, hope, trust, and unconditional commitment to Christ a commitment requiring that regardless of what passion we may feel, we must be pure. Chastity presupposes not taking lightly any act or thought that is not appropriate to the kind of commitment you have to God. To equate any and every personal sexual desire as natural, healthy, and God-given is a powerful lie. God does not give desires that cannot be fulfilled according to His standards of holiness, wholeness, and purity. Sexual purity is one of the foremost means of safeguarding a marriage from behaviors that pollute, corrupt, infect, or destroy it physically, emotionally, or spiritually.

Purity means freedom from contamination, from anything that would spoil the taste or the pleasure, reduce the power, or in any way adulterate what a thing is meant to be. Within marriage, sexual union is natural, healthy, and pleasurable not only for the moment, but for all of life together. Sexual intimacy is natural, in the sense in which the original Designer created it to be. When virginity and purity are no longer protected and prized, there is dullness, monotony, and sheer boredom. By trying to grab fulfillment everywhere, you find it nowhere.

Purity before marriage consists of giving ourselves to and for each other in obedience to God. Passion must be held by principle. The principle is love not merely erotic, sentimental, or sexual feeling. There is no other way to control passion and no other route to purity and joy. If you choose to avoid the sin of sexual immorality, that is God's ideal; but if you have already given away your virginity, the message of the gospel proclaims New Birth, a new beginning, and a new creation (2 Cor. 5:17).

The Scriptures have strong admonitions about abstaining from both adultery and fornication. Paul made special mention of sins related to the body. He clearly stated that the body of the believer belongs to the Lord (1 Cor. 6:19). It is His temple (1 Cor. 3:16). A believing woman is to use both her body and spirit to bring glory and praise to God (1 Cor. 6:20). Fornication engaging in sexual activity with a person outside the commitment of marriage is a sin against your own body. Physically, this sin can reap diseases from which those who keep themselves sexually pure are protected. This sin also can reap emotional distress that those who practice purity do not experience. Spiritually, those who habitually practice this sin will miss the fullness of His blessings. Fornication can describe harlotry and prostitution (Rev. 2:14, 20) and various other forms of unchastely (John 8:41; Acts 15:20; 1 Cor. 5:1).

Masturbation is defined as the self-stimulation or manipulation of the genital organs, often to the point of sexual climax or orgasm. Some consider it a means of reducing excessive sexual tension when the normal sexual activity of married life is unavailable or as an alternative for promiscuity or fornication. On the other hand, such self-gratification may originate in lustful fantasies for selfish pleasure. Alpha women in Christ should be aware of the danger of masturbating while fantasizing about a desired but inappropriate sexual partner, which Jesus equates with actual commission of sexual intercourse (Matt. 5:27, 28).

Scripture neither explicitly condones nor condemns masturbation. Jesus does not mention it, nor does not mention it, nor does Paul include it in his list vile passions (Rom. 1:26-31). Nevertheless, the moral and psychological ramifications of masturbation can prove disruptive to a relationship with God as well as others, particularly in a marriage. Certainly masturbation does not fulfill God's plan for sexual intimacy between husband and wife (Gen. 2:24). Overall, Scripture advocates an ever-present awareness that human beings are more than sexual or physical. God is interested in our wholeness, which encompasses every area of life.

Chapter 71
Competition: When Sisters Fight

Competition in the sense of a common struggle for the same objective can be a healthy thing. It can inspire alpha women in Christ to study harder and run faster. To be challenged and pushed to reach a goal is not wrong in itself. But when sin starts to edge its way into the competition, the goal of personal achievement is distorted into an obsession to show up someone else. Such competition can move our eyes from focus on the intended goal and instead make us dwell upon comparing ourselves to another. This makes competition wrong (2 Cor. 10:12).

Competition has become so commonplace in our culture that we assume it is acceptable to God in any form. Scripture does not support that position. The ideal advocate in the Bible is cooperation, agreement, and unity among believers. Several metaphors are used to describe such cooperation among believers: we are a "building" with parts jointly fitted together, a "body of Christ," a "chosen generation," and a "royal priesthood" (1 Cor. 12:27; Eph. 2:20-22; 1 Pet. 2:9). The bestowal of the Holy Spirit upon the early church came as those gathered reached "one accord in one place" (Acts 2:1).The Apostle Paul spoke on numerous occasions of the need for unity of spirit (Eph. 4:3).

When Jesus came to visit, Mary and Martha started using their gifts of service. Mary sat at Jesus' feet, loving and being loved by Him. Martha, a practical "doer," started preparing food and place to rest. Martha looked away from her goal of serving Christ and began to evaluate Mary's performance. Both women were serving in meaningful ways. The problem came when Martha, in her anxiety, overlooked the fact that she and her sister were both on the same team and began to sit in judgment of her sister (Luke 10:41, 42).

The gift of the Spirit are to work in harmony with one another as the Holy Spirit directs, so that the entire body of alpha women in Christ is built up (1

Cor. 12:7, 11, 12). We are responsible for one another's welfare; we are to pray for one another; we are called to be one-minded and to live in peace (2 Cor. 13:11). Indeed, when arguments arise, we are to give preference to one another or to defer for the sake of achieving harmony (Rom. 12:10).

Chapter 72
Spiritual Gifts: Equipped for Service

Spiritual gifts are special abilities given to believers for ministry and service. God is the divine source of all gifts (1 Pet. 4:10), and His gifts are very diverse (1 Cor. 12:4, 5). These spiritual gifts are not given only to the elite. Each alpha woman in Christ receives at least one spiritual gift (1 Cor. 12:7-11). All spiritual gifts are to be used for Christian service, not for personal edification (Eph. 4:11-16).

The gifts of the "Spirit" are unique manifestations of the Holy Spirit. While natural or inherited talents are also God-given, spiritual gifts are not dependent upon genetic codes and are specifically intended to serve others. Whereas the "fruit of the Spirit" refers to the character of a believer, the "gifts of the Spirit" describe the service of a believer. At the time of salvation, a believer receives the gift of the Holy Spirit's presence; then throughout life she uses specific spiritual gifts given by the Spirit for the benefit of others.

The New Testament identifies a variety of spiritual gifts. Paul's listing of about twenty different spiritual gifts is not to be considered comprehensive but rather presents examples of the diversity of potential gifts available for service.

Some of the gifts are employed in serving, others in teaching, and all for edifying the church. Most important in the eyes of the Lord is not the particular gift but rather an individual's faithfulness to use the gift bestowed unselfishly and for the edification of the church. One of the greatest challenges an alpha woman in Christ faces is that of discovering and using her specific spiritual gifts. Personal Bible and prayer can help an alpha woman in Christ unwrap unique gifts of the Spirit. Various inventors are also available to assess spiritual gifts. Since God has carefully selected specific spiritual gifts for each of His children, each Christian is responsible for discovering, developing, and using her personal gifts for God's service.

Chapter 73
Access to God: A Personal Encounter

Under the old covenant, human access to God was limited. Only the high priest once a year could enter the Most Holy Place to meet directly with the Lord. New Covenant believers, however, regarded the tearing of the veil, the thick curtain that separated the holy place from the Most Holy Place, at the time of the Crucifixion as a sign that all could freely come to God through Christ Jesus (Matt. 27:51-54; Eph. 2:13).

Prior to the death of Jesus on the Cross...

- Only priests (of the Levite tribe) could offer gifts and sacrifices;
- Only Hebrews could be called the sons and daughters of the Lord;
- Only those who kept the Day of Atonement were considered in right relationship with God;
- Only those who fully knew and followed the Law could be called righteous.

After the death of Jesus on the Cross...
Whoever calls on the name of the Lord shall be saved (Rom. 10:12-13);

- A person can be called a child of God regardless of race, sex, or social status (Gal. 3:26-29; 4:1-7; Col. 3:9-11);
- Whoever believers in Christ shall be counted as righteous (1 John 2:29) and shall inherit everlasting life (John 3:16);
- All who believe can make the ultimate sacrifice to God, which is to do His will with all of your heart, mind, and soul (Rom. 12:1; Heb. 10:7).

Chapter 74
Fatherhood of God: My Heavenly Father

In recent years, much discussion has been given to the practice of referring to God as "Father" (Jer. 3:19), and this was the term Jesus used in addressing Him (John 17). The Fatherhood of God is not merely one of many suitable God metaphors. It is in a class of its own, what scholars would label as an analogy. The title "Father" not only tells us what God does or what some aspect of His character is like; rather, it identifies more of who He actually is. The same cannot be said of biblical God metaphors such as "tree," "door," "rock," "mother hen," or "mistress of the house."

True Fatherhood is grounded in the basis of God's being in the basis of God the Father relating to the Son and the Spirit. Human fatherhood is but an imperfect symbol of this transcendent reality. The Fatherhood of God is not inconsequential or alterable, for it is the primary basis by which God has determined that alpha women in Christ will relate to Him: "I will receive you, and will be a Father unto you, and ye shall be my sons and daughters, saith the Lord Almighty" (2 Cor. 6:17, 18).

Chapter 75
Fruit of the Spirit

In both the Old and New Testaments, peace is described as the result of having a right relationship to God and with others (Rom. 5:1, 2). Spiritual peace describes a sense of well-being and fulfillment that comes from God and is dependent on His presence alone (Gal. 5:22). Inner spiritual peace is experienced by any believer who walks in the Spirit despite surrounding turmoil. The true "peace of God" protects the hearts and minds of alpha woman in Christ from worry, fear, and anxiety. It transcends all logic or rationale (Phil. 4:7). The God of Peace who offers salvation also promises His presence and power in the lives of His children. His presence creates in us quiet confidence, regardless of circumstances, people, or things.

Though impossible to comprehend fully, true peace is a fruit of the Holy Spirit (Gal. 5:22) and a part of the "whole armor of God" (Eph. 6:11, 13). According to the apostle Paul, our understanding and experiencing of the gospel produces peace that allows us to walk boldly into spiritual battle (Eph. 6:11, 13) and to survive all manner of difficulty and danger. The alpha woman in Christ receives peace from God as a virtue of holy living and a protection from evil forces. Where the peace of God is present, there is no room for worry.

Chapter 76
Attributes of God: He is Long-Suffering

God's judgment is sure (Rev. 19:2, 11). God is called "long-suffering" because He does not execute judgment immediately. He waits (Is. 42:14-16), not to see what will happen He knows what will happen; not to see more clearly He sees perfectly; not to gain more information He knows everything. God waits because His priority is self-revelation, not judgment.

Longsuffering is not the absence of anger but being slow to anger (Ps. 145:8). God's longsuffering shows an infinite amount of power, mercy, patience, and love all of which He has in abundance (Num. 14:18). God, for a time, tolerates insults, rejection, and indifference in order to draw people to repentance (Rom. 2:4). His longsuffering is linked with His great compassion and becomes active in order to draw us to Himself (2Pet. 3:9).

Chapter 77
Disabilities: The Value of
Special-Needs Children

Physical and mental health handicaps are forever a part of this fallen world. Most families have been affected by disabilities heightened. When a mother is disabled, the children can learn very early that caring for such a woman is a privilege. Because she cannot run to catch and discipline her children, they have to learn to obey her instantly because of their love and respect for her.

When a child with a handicap is born into a home, the family has an opportunity to turn to the Lord in a fresh way, realizing that though God allowed the handicap to occur, He would in some way work it to the good of all involved (Rom. 8:28). Such a child demands unconditional love.

Through the handicap of one, others can learn lessons:

- Patience waiting to see God's final work (Is. 40:31; Thess.5:14);
- Gratitude being thankful for any small gain made (Eph. 5:20);
- Faith learning to depend absolutely upon God and His Word whatever the circumstances (2 Cor. 12:9);
- Kindness toward others accepting them and responding to them in loving kindness (Heb. 12:2).

Ministering to those with disabilities teaches us lessons that could never be learned in any other way, and God blesses in the process (Matt. 25:40). Through the weakness found in disabilities, the Lord's strength is made perfect (Heb. 11:34). Those who lovingly serve the disabled are made strong in the love of God. The Lord told us to love one another and to bear the burdens of on another (Gal. 6:2). There is value in service to those with disabilities and much to be learned by both those who serve and those who are being served.

This value is primarily found in being drawn close to our Savior who Himself set the example for us.

Chapter 78
Prejudice: Impeding the Kingdom's Growth

Prejudice denies alpha women in Christ free fellowship, thereby impeding access to the spiritual gifts God has placed throughout the body of Christ. The different gifts and their varied administrations are given so that all the people of God might be made stronger (1 Cor. 12:7).

Jews and Gentiles had been longtime adversaries when God directed Peter, a Jew, to go to the home of Cornelius, a Gentile. Though reluctant, Peter obeyed and went to the Gentile home and preached, and the entire family believed (Acts 10:28-35). Peter marveled at God's grace. Peter's visit initiated open access to the gospel of Jesus Christ of all.

Alpha women in Christ are wise to use caution when segregating themselves according to ethnic, gender, or socio-economic differences. All alpha women are one in Christ (Gal. 3:28). Communication and shared fellowship are perhaps the greatest weapons against prejudice because they weaken hasty, harsh judgments and clear the way for compassion.

Chapter 79
Employment: Choosing a Profession

The Bible provides numerous examples of professions and jobs. In most cases, professions in the Old Testament were "inherited" passed down from father to son or mother to daughter in something of a mentoring manner or apprenticeship relationship. Occasionally, a person's special talents in a particular area or the call of God on the person's life were noted, and that person then was singled out for a unique position, such as when Deborah became a judge of Israel (Judg. 4:4, 5).

In the New Testament, women and men enjoyed much more autonomy in "choosing" a line of work or a profession. Lydia was a notable businesswoman in the textile industry (Acts 16:14); Dorcas was a well-respected seamstress (Acts 9:39); and Priscilla worked in the tent-making trade (Acts 18:2, 3).

The understanding of the New Testament believers, however, was that their entire lives were subject to God's command and direction, including their choices of careers. The Holy Spirit was to be trusted both for direction and timing. The idea of a "career path" was not regarded as something that a person must engineer on her own, but something that flowed naturally from a person's talents and abilities and in response to opportunities that arose. An alpha woman in Christ to be motivated in your work by a desire to use your abilities to their fullest for the glory of God rather than being motivated by positions on corporate ladders, work incentives, higher salaries, or cultural standards of prestige and status. The Bible clearly warns against worshiping the work of your own hands or exalting that which you have created or earned to the place of supreme honor in your life (Ps. 115:1-8; Jer. 25:6, 7).

Chapter 80
Racial Relations: No Respect of Persons

The task of each alpha woman in Christ is twofold to proclaim the gospel and to love her neighbor. Jesus Christ demonstrates that racial relations must be based on love (Mark 2:15-17; 7:25-30) and that the gospel is intended for all races, tribes, and nations (Luke 2:32; Rev. 14:6). The Bible does not contain any clear definition of race, referring instead to nations, tribes, tongues, and peoples. Yet racial prejudices appear to be intolerable. The Lord showed His displeasure by disciplining Miriam for her criticism of Moses' Ethiopian wife (Num. 12:1-15). Jonah was disciplined when he refused to take his ministry to those of another culture (Jon. 1:12). Peter, after opening the "door of faith unto the Gentiles," was admonished when his behavior did not exemplify grace (Acts 10:15; Gal. 2:11-18). We must avoid the idea that God approves any mistreatment according to race.

The Bible contains no justification that the people of one race are superior to those of another. Eve is called the "mother of all living" (Gen. 3:20), and all are created in the image of God (Gen. 1:26, 27). All people are under the power of sin and are sinners, and everyone falls short of the glory of God and needs redemption (Rom. 3:23). Jesus Christ did not die on the Cross exclusively for one group but for all (John 1:29; Rom. 3:23). Jesus Christ did not die on the Cross exclusively for one group but for all (John 1:29; Rom. 8:32). God does not respect persons according to their outward status or condition, and neither should His children (Luke 6:43-45; James 2:1).

The evaluative question must be, "Would God be pleased with the way I treat those of other races? As alpha women of Christ, we must exemplify His standard of love for all people," (2 Cor. 5:29; John 15:12).

Chapter 81
Women's Ministries:
Coworkers in the Kingdom

Women in the New Testament were not spectators. They played an active, vibrant, and vital-role in the day-to-day function of the church. God poured out His Spirit upon both sons and daughters (Joel 2:28; Acts 2:17, 18), and Spirit-empowered women ministered using the full spectrum of gifts. Besides evangelism, prophecy, teaching, and discipleship, women were involved in countless other ministries, together with service to their families (1 Tim. 5:10), according to their respective spiritual gifts (Acts 1:14; 12:12; 1 Cor. 12:8-10; 1 Tim. 5:5; Philem. 2).

Women were an active part of the assembly in Philippi (Acts 16:11-15) and were involved in the establishment of churches in Thessalonica (Acts 17:4) and Berea (Acts 17:12). Paul often referred to women as his "fellow laborers." He specifically acknowledged Mary (Rom. 16:6), Tryphena, Tryphosa, and Persis (Rom. 16:2), Euodia and Syntyche (Phil. 4:2), and Priscilla (Rom. 16:3) as women who had labored hard for the gospel. The coming of the kingdom revolutionized the involvement of ordinary people in the work of God. Whether Jew or Greek, slave or free, male or female kingdom ministry became the responsibility of all.

Chapter 82
Women's Ministries:
Women in Evangelism

Jesus affirmed the ministry of women in evangelism. This was most evident in His interaction with the Samaritan woman at the well of Sychar (John 4:1-30). Culturally, Jews and Samaritans did not associate with each other. Furthermore, for a rabbit to speak to a woman in public was considered improper. Christ's regard for this woman was therefore truly revolutionary. After their meeting, she returned to her city and presented her witness. Many believed in Him because of her testimony. At that time, woman were not considered reliable witnesses; yet Christ chose a woman as His witness.

God chose women as the first witnesses of Christ's Resurrection (Matt. 28:1-8), and they were entrusted with Christ's first post-Resurrection message to His disciples (John 20:15-18). The coming of the Spirit reinforced the role of women in evangelism. Women, together with men, were empowered to be witnesses to the ends of the earth (Acts 1:8). The establishment of the Philippian church involved women (Acts 16:11-15), and women were also involved in spreading the gospel in Berea (Acts 17:12). New Testament women, along with men, were commissioned to be the "light of the world" and were thus extensively involved in the ministry of evangelism (Matt. 5:14-16).

Chapter 83
Weddings: A Public Commitment

In Bible times, the period of engagement (or betrothal) was spent in preparation the groom preparing a home for his bride and the bride preparing herself and her trousseau. When the time came for the marriage to be consummated, the groom went to the bride's home (often at an unannounced time) to accompany her to his home where they met friends of the two families, as arranged by the groom, not the bride (Judg. 14:5-11; Matt. 25:1-13). Wedding celebrations generally lasted a week, during which time the bride and groom dressed and were treated as royalty amidst festivities and the presentation of gifts (Gen. 29:27; Judg. 14:12-18; John 2:1-11).

In the modern era, weddings range from formal, solemn ceremonies to informal, private gatherings. The type of ceremony is not necessarily important, but these biblical criteria are:

1. The marriage should be established in the name of the Lord Jesus (Mark 10:9), and
2. Thanks should be given to God (Col. 3:17). A wedding should be a time of worship and should celebrate each marriage partner's commitment grounded in the love of God.

Weddings are much more than beautiful gowns, crowds of people, and expensive decorating. A wedding is a time of COMMITMENT. It should include worship and giving thanks to God as well as the celebrating of the wonderful blessing God has given both the bride and groom. The wedding ceremony is an appropriate time to reflect on the example of unconditional love, which God has demonstrated (Rom. 5:8). The couple should commit to follow the Lord in their home no matter what circumstances arise and "until death do us part" (Matt. 19:6). The importance of this permanency of the union grows out of the fact that the vows are not merely between one man and one woman but include the heavenly Father Himself, and also because such commitment is modeled after Christ's commitment to the church (Eph. 5:21-33).

Chapter 84
God's Refreshing Word

When The Word spoke the world into being in Genesis, it was Jesus, in the mystery of the Trinity, speaking the world into existence. When "the Word of the Lord came to Hosea," it was Jesus, in the mystery of the Trinity, speaking to Hosea. When the law was given to Moses, it was Jesus communicating to the heart of His people. Not only does the Word include God's supportive presence among His people, but it contains the Law: the words, and the holy judgment of God as seen in the Torah. (The Torah is the first five books of Moses: Genesis through Deuteronomy).

This communication aspect of the Word has both a terrible and wonderful side. It can fell terrible when it convicts us of sin. It can seem harsh when you read of someone being cast out into the outer darkness where there is weeping and gnashing of teeth. It can be wonderful when we hear how wide and high His love is, when He tells us He will never leave us, and when He promises us that one day, we will no longer weep.

Because God is always good and just, what may seem terrible is not. It is a holy mystery. The picture of Jesus coming on a white horse one day with fire in His eyes and a sword in His mouth causes us to tremble. And yet, that day is when He is waging war against all the enemies of His bride, because He is holy and just. We have come to love this picture of Jesus because we see the sword being used on our behalf and in our defense. The sword, Paul told us in Ephesians 6, represents the Word of God, and we can use it, as well, to defeat our spiritual enemies. When the enemy comes, and he will, we can use the sword of the Spirit, the Word of God, against him.

Jesus, as the Word, is here with us and is filled with wisdom, power, and comfort. And as He, through His Spirit and His Word, falls upon hearts eager to receive, He cannot help but produce fruit. Hosea talked about the Lord coming to us "like the rain, like the latter and former rain to the earth" (6:3).

Likewise, Isaiah extends the analogy, and in his picture is an exciting truth: "For as the rain comes down, and the snow from heaven, and do not return there, but water the earth, and make it bring forth and bud, that it may give seed to the sower and bread to the eater, so shall My word be that goes forth from My mouth; it shall not return to Me void, but it shall accomplish what I please, and it shall prosper in the thing for which I sent" (55:10, 11).

Chapter 85
Financial Planning: Wise Money Management

Good financial planning is a part of wise stewardship. To be truly effective steward, you must believe unequivocally that the money being managed is someone else's money God's money. Having this perspective gives an alpha woman in Christ the freedom to use finances as a tool to accomplish God's purposes, recognizing that no one comes into this world with any possessions, and no one will leave with anything (Eccl. 5:15).

God has entrusted each alpha woman in Christ with certain resources. Money is something that God uses to test your ability to handle properly the other gifts He desires to give you (Luke 16:11). One day He will ask for an accounting of how you managed the resources He has given you (Luke 19:11-26). A wife who manages resources wisely is a blessing to her husband and family (Prov. 31:28).

An alpha woman in Christ is Wise to remember:

- The earth and all its fullness is the Lord's (Ps. 24:1). Every resource, even money, is His, and you are simply stewards of His resources.
- Avoid an overly consumptive lifestyle. The Bible teaches moderation in all things (1 Cor. 9:25).
- Avoid debt (Prov. 22:7; Rom. 13:8).
- Maintain a savings program (Prov. 12:11).
- Set long-term goals (Prov. 13:22).

Chapter 86
Forgiveness: Extended Mercy to Others

When someone comes seeking your forgiveness, an alpha woman in Christ has obligation to grant forgiveness and extend mercy even if the person has sinned may have been (Matt. 18:21, 22; Luke 17:4; Eph. 4:32; Col. 3:12, 13). Your forgiveness of others is a prerequisite for your receiving God's forgiveness (Matt. 6:14, 15; Luke 11:4; James 2:13). God does indeed forgive us (Ps. 32:1-5; 103:12; 130:3, 4; Is. 43:25; Jer. 31:34; Eph. 1:7; Col. 1:14; 2:13). We forgive others, if we do not want to disobey God and break our fellowship with Him (Matt. 6:14, 15; Mark 11:25, 26; Luke 17:3, 4). No less important is the willingness for one who blames God for wrongs experienced to remember that the Lord does not direct evil against us, though He may choose to allow us to go through a trial resulting from our own sinful choices or from the sinfulness of the world in which we live (Gen. 50:20; Deut. 32:4; Rom. 8:28, 38, 39). Finally, we must be willing to forgive ourselves since we are finite beings and since our failures often open the door for His glory and provide the environment for our own growth (Phil. 3:12-16).

Love is the prime ingredient in forgiveness (Prov. 10:12). Often the one wounded must forgive with an act of the will, giving time for working through feelings and experiencing healing. Forgiveness comes with the removal of past offenses from the mind (Phil. 3:13), followed by meditation upon Scripture (Ps. 119:157-160), giving over to God our hurts (1 Pet. 2:21-23), praying for the offender (1 Sam 12:23; Matt. 5:44), and serving as a willing channel for God's grace. God has promised that He will take care of all judgment so that revenge is not an option (Rom. 12:19-21).

Meaningful forgiveness demands thought and planning. Forgiveness is the willingness to search for new solutions. Forgiveness insists on a new way neither yours nor theirs but one mutually acceptable. You must be concerned with seeking forgiveness only for your wrong (Ps. 51:1-4). An alpha woman in Christ must remember that a forgiving attitudes does not excuse self (Gen. 3:12), defend self (Gen. 3:10), or accuse another (Gen. 3:13). Seeking forgiveness frees you to receive God's mercy (Prov. 28:13). Showing mercy by a forgiving spirit brings blessings from God and gratitude from the one forgiven. A forgiving spirit brings good to yourself (Prov. 11:17) and to others (15:23).

Chapter 87
Stewardship: Accountable to God

Accountability is an integral part of daily living. It is the requirement of the giver and the responsibility of the recipient (1 Cor. 4:2). The employed are accountable to the employer, the married to spouse and family, the citizen to society, and all of us to God (Rom. 14:12). Jesus tells the parable about a rich man whose steward was accused of wasting his master's goods (Luke 16:1, 2). The steward was summoned and told, "Give an account of thy stewardship." While this steward was able to act quickly and wisely to set things in order, Jesus used this story to make an important point: "He that is faithful in that which is least is faithful also in much: and he that is unjust in the least is unjust also in much."

God is Creator and Owner of all things (Deut. 10:14; Ps. 24:1, 2). All that is possessed comes as a gift from His hand (Acts 17:25). Our master Jesus Christ will ultimately require an accounting of each person's stewardship (2 Cor. 5:10).

Christian stewards can be prepared for that day of accountability by taking seriously their stewardship responsibilities. Whether the managed resource is time, talent, or money, the steward should endeavor to avoid waste, maximize return, and, above all, assure that the investment is pleasing to God.

Time should be used wisely; talents should be shared to edify others glorify God; money should be spent carefully and given responsibly. Our drive to execute these requirements faithfully comes from having an acute awareness of our personal accountability to God (1 Pet. 4:10).

Chapter 88
Children: Parenting Adult Children

In the parable of the prodigal, Jesus provided a pattern for a healthy relationship between adult children and their parents (Luke 15:11-32);

- The father acknowledged the independence of both sons even against his better judgment in the case of the younger (vv.12, 31).
- Rather than demanding childlike obedience from the elder son, who protested the generous welcome extended to his wayward brother, the father reasoned with him as one adult to another (vv. 31, 32).
- The father allowed both sons to make their own decisions and bear the consequences of their actions.
- The father extended to each son unconditional, forgiving love (vv. 21-24, 31).

While even Jesus felt compelled to assert His adult independence (Matt. 12:46-50), adulthood does not preclude loving interdependence between children and parents. Noah's adult sons benefited from his protection (Gen. 6:18-22). Judah attempted to spare his elderly father Jacob from heartbreak (Gen, 44:19-34). While enduring the Cross Jesus made provision for the care of His mother (John 19:26, 27).

The loving bond between parent and child is not to be broken by aging, inevitable transfer of residence, and subsequent realignment of loyalties. Rather it remains as an enduring commitment between parent and offspring from birth to death to be available to each other and responsive to each other's need (Prov. 4:3-6, 10-13).

Chapter 89
Poverty: Providing for Those in Need

Those counted among the poor were the needy, the weak, and those who were dependent the orphans and the widows who were usually in the lower social classes and in need of protection from abuse and neglect. Virtually every prophet of the Old Testament prophesied against those who wrongfully oppressed the poor (Jer. 22:13-16).

God provided for the poor through His principle of gleaning. Landowners were instructed to leave the remaining grain around the outer perimeters of the fields for the poor to gather (Lev. 19:10; Ruth 2:2, 15, 16). The courts, too, were admonished to deal justly with the poor (Ex. 23:6, 7).

Jesus himself was born into a poor family and called the poor His brethren (Matt. 25:40). The early church recognized the importance of caring for widows (Acts 6:1-6) and took offerings to meet their needs (Rom. 15:26). Alpha women in Christ are admonished to be mindful of the poor (Gal. 2:10). Every believer will be held accountable for how she has responded to those in need. One of the ways to judge our relationship to Christ is to observe how we respond to the hungry, the thirsty, the naked, the stranger, and the prisoner (Matt. 25:31-46). Compassion is regarded as evidence of the presence of Christ inside the heart (1 Pet. 3:8; 1 John 3:16, 17).

God often chooses to reveal Himself to the world through the poor (James 2:5); rarely do the rich, great, and noble hear His call or choose His path (Matt. 19:16-24). Paul concluded that if the Lord used only the wealthy to extend His cause, critics would credit those people and their resources instead of God with the good that was done through them (1 Cor. 1:26).

The first step to having your physical needs met is to become "poor in spirit," recognizing that every heart separated from God is in spiritual poverty, which is far more tragic than physical poverty (Matt. 5:3). The Lord has promised to provide freely for His children (Rom. 8:32).

Chapter 90
An Infirm Woman

Only Luke mentions this bent-over woman who had spent the previous eighteen years staring at the floor, unable to stand or sit, or even to straighten her crooked back. Jesus and His disciples had traveled through her city in Perea on their way from Galilee to Judea. They entered the synagogue on the Sabbath to teach.

Jesus had deep compassion for this tragic woman. He touched her and healed her. When the ruler of the synagogue rebuked Jesus for the unlawful Sabbath healing, Jesus firmly exposed the inconsistency of those who would lead an ox to water on the Sabbath, yet oppose the healing of an afflicted woman.

How odd that Jesus refers to her as "a daughter of Abraham," since such a description is usually reserved for the "sons" of Abraham. In front of all the upright religious folk, Jesus gave this humble woman a place of honor when He affirmed that she, too, belonged to the family of Abraham. After Jesus' tender touch, for the first time in eighteen years, this "daughter of Abraham" straightened her back, stretched to her full height, and, among the sons of Abraham, who perhaps now hung their heads in shame, she held her head high to the glory of God. Nothing honors the Savior any more than a heart of gratitude and a spirit of praise.

Chapter 91
Education: Studying at the Feet of Jesus

Mary of Bethany is noted among the first women of the Christ era as one who pursued a theological education at the feet of Jesus. Luke thoughtfully records that Mary sat at Jesus' feet and heard His word in a time when it was highly untraditional for a woman to be taught, especially by an esteemed rabbi. When Mary was criticized, Jesus Himself commended her for choosing the better way (Luke 10:38-42).

A woman need not enroll in a Bible college or seminary to sit at Jesus' feet and hear His word; but a ministry could be enhanced and extended by formal theological education, which provides a systematic study of God and the way He relates to us. When the Lord calls a woman to a Christian vocation, she should devote herself to the same high standards of training as she would to prepare for any other vocation. Alpha women in Christ dare not offer less to the Lord's work than we would to a secular profession. When intellectual integrity and academic excellence are pursued with a heart fully devoted to the Lord, God is glorified, and that is the ultimate goal of theological education.

Chapter 92
The Homeless: A Lowly Estate

The homeless considered the most destitute of all the poor, are positioned to bring great honor to God. Their lowly state makes it possible for God to raise them up with great visibility His life. Yet at His death, which appeared to be His lowest point, He was highly exalted above all men (Phil. 2:5-10).

Jesus used extreme cases to reveal to the world the extent of the Father's grace, mercy, power, and loving kindness. His giving sight to the man born blind (John 9:6-7); His raising Lazarus, dead four days, from the grave (John 11:38-44); His forgiveness of well-known prostitutes and adulteress (John 8:1-12); and His calling Saul, the murdered and persecutor of the church, to be an apostle all serve as examples of God's promise to lift up the down-trodden and to bring satisfaction to those in need (Ex. 3:7; Prov. 3:34).

In a spiritual sense, all are homeless on this earth. The believer's true home remains yet to be seen; it is not one made with human hands (Ps. 39:12; Heb. 11:13-16). Alpha women in Christ are always to be sensitive and responsive to those who are weaker (Ps. 8:23, 4; Prov. 31:8, 9; Rom. 15:1).

Chapter 93
Adolescence: The In-Between Stage

This in-between stage of rapid physical, mental, and spiritual growth is potentially a time during which young people begin making more of their own choices. Scripture offers examples of teens making choices, ranging from the wise choices of Jesus at age twelve to the poor choices of the prodigal son.

During this transition time, parents move toward letting go, recognize that the child has been given in stewardship from the Lord (1 Sam. 1:11; Ps. 127:3-5). This letting go gives adolescents room for growth in an atmosphere of parental guidance and influence as well as accountability (Rom. 14:12; 1 Cor. 10:13). Parents watch their teens move from parent-control to self-control and then hopefully t God-control.

In the midst of this letting go, parents of adolescents must also remember that God created each child uniquely; each must be reared with loving attention and encouragement to her particular talents, gifts, and personality (Prov. 3:27), with consistent discipline to lead the child God's way (Prov. 22:6; 27:5), with the faithful example of a consistent Christ like lifestyle (Deut. 6:7-9; 2 Cor. 3:2, 3), with godly counsel and advice (Prov. 12:15; 19:20), and with undergirding in prayer (1 Sam. 12:23).

Teens need to realize that they are experiencing a great time of change. They should cling to the spiritual values they know to be true, exercise patience with self and others, and recognize that increased authority over their own lives means responsibility for honoring commitments and making wise choices. God commands children to honor their parents and to obey God's laws, regardless of age (Eph. 6:1-3).

Chapter 94
Servanthood: Becoming Great in Jesus' Way

To study biblical servanthood is to study Jesus. Jesus' only Master was the Father (Is. 53:4-6, 10-12; John 4:34). He served others because that was the Father's assignment (1 John 17:4-12). Jesus assumed the title of "servant," and this title is incorporated within the messianic prophecies in which He is described as the servant of the Lord (Is. 42:1-7; 49:1-7; 50:4-11; 52:13-53:12). In fact, Jesus understood Himself as "the fulfillment of Isaiah's suffering servant." Even before He went to the Cross, Jesus made sure the disciples understood servanthood. They watched in amazement as He redefined leadership by taking a towel and washing their dirty feet. In His life, biblical leadership and servanthood were synonymous. Many divinely appointed leaders described themselves as "servants."

Normally servanthood is placed at the bottom rung of the ladder of success, with authority at the top. Jesus, in a revolutionary way, flipped the ladder right side up. In imitating Him, servants neither lose their identities nor become doormats; they become great (Mark 10:43).

Many women rendered service: Ruth served her mother-in-law Naomi (Ruth 1:16, 17); Esther served her people in one of their darkest hours (Esth. 4:16); the prophetess Anna served the Lord in the temple (Luke 2:37); Mary of Bethany anointed the Savior with costly oil (Matt. 26:6-10). Women followed Him faithfully even to the Cross in order to minister to His needs (Matt. 27: 55).

There is no shame in biblical servanthood (Is. 49:23), which carries the imprimatur of the Lord's confidence (Is. 42:1). Such a servant works with a gentle, sensitive spirit (v. 2) and refuses to quit under suffering (v. 3). The God-honoring servant ultimately does not fail (v. 4), presents worthy goals (v. 4), is undergirded by the Lord (v. 6; Is. 49:5), and is rewarded with a fulfilling ministry (Is. 42:7; 49:4, 6) that glorifies the Lord (Is. 49:3). The followers of

Jesus should be easily recognized (Mark 10:43; John 13:13-16). They will be humbly ready for service in every way (Eph. 6:5-9; Phil. 2:6-8; Col. 3:17).

Chapter 95
Enabling Codependency in Action

Enabling is codependency in action. An enabler is someone who responds to another's problem by attempting to take care of the situation by making things all right. Feeling that the other person's problem is most likely her fault, an enabler allows the behavior to determine her worth. Only when she is doing for others does she feel "I'm somebody, I'm appreciated, I have value." This over-developed sense of responsibility makes it hard to let go and allow others to take responsibility for their own behavior and problems.

The solution to the quicksand of enabling is found in a new understanding of what God says about your relationships with others and about who God is and who you are. Scripture makes it clear that no one is responsible for the actions of others (Rom. 14:12). When the rich young ruler came to Jesus (Mark 10:17-22), Jesus spoke truth to him, then let him make his own decision. He did not attempt to follow the young man or manipulate his actions though He loved him dearly.

Letting go is hard. However, understanding that God alone is the Great Shepherd (John 10:11) and that He does His job well (Is. 40:11) makes it possible for you to release even one greatly loved to the Lord. The enabler, most of all, needs to understand who she is in Christ (Eph. 1:17, 18). She is of great value because God loves her not because of what she does but for who she is as His beloved daughter. The Lord loved her before she had a chance to accomplish or fail at anything; and as a new creation in Christ Jesus, she is holy and blameless in His eyes (Eph. 1:4). God's love and mercy toward her are rich and great (Eph. 2:4, 5), and she is His child because God wills for her to be so, not because she has earned favor on her own merit (Eph. 1:5).

Chapter 96
Touching: An Expression of Love

The woman appeared out of nowhere. "If I may but touch his garment," she whispered under her breath. She pushed her way through the crowd and touched the hem of Jesus' robe. And the woman, who had suffered a continuous blood flow for twelve years, was healed. While touching and kissing were common in biblical days, Levitical Law forbade many forms of touching. A Hebrew could not touch an unclean animal (Lev. 11:8), a woman following childbirth (Lev. 12:2), a victim of leprosy (Lev. 13:11), or a woman in her menstrual cycle (Lev. 15:19).

Jesus, motivated by a love that transcended the Law, frequently touched others. He touched a leprous man (Mark 1:41), a blind man's eyes (John 9:6), the dead body of Jairus' daughter (Mark 5:41), and a deaf-mute's tongue (Mark 7:33). He gave no thought to Himself as He reached out to others. Jesus also allowed others to touch Him. A woman "who was a sinner" washed and kissed His feet (Luke 7:37, 38). A bleeding woman touched His robe's hem (Matt.9:20, 21). Jesus often healed and imparted His compassion through touch because touching communicates empathy, affection, healing, and affirmation. Those who have felt His touch must reach out in turn to touch others. There is no better way to feel a person's heartbeat than to embrace that one in a holy hug!

Chapter 97
Leisure: A Time to Rest and Play

The Bible speaks in a negative way about idleness (Prov. 6:6-11; 1 Tim. 5:13), referring to those who are lazy by such loathsome words as "slothful," "sluggard," and "slack hand" and very positively about labor and work (Luke 10:7; 1 Cor. 3:8, 9; Eph. 4:28, 1 Thes. 4:11). Given the admonition that we are to work six days and rest one (Ex. 34:21), we might conclude that the Bible is about all work and no fun. That is far from the truth! Jesus expected His disciples to "come ye yourselves apart" periodically for rest (Mark 6:31), and Scripture has repeated references to the benefits of "making merry" (Prov. 15:13, 15; 17:22; Luke 15:32).

The Bible speaks of more than seventy days a year in which "no servile work" is to be done (Lev. 23:7, 8): the seven-day feasts that mark Passover, Tabernacles, and Weeks, as well as the Feast of Trumpets, and every Sabbath day! In addition to rest and prayer, leisure days in the Bible are associated with food, gift-giving, singing, and great joy (Rev. 11:10).

A time of rest from work is advocated for those who are experiencing grief (Matt. 14:10-13), those who are seeking spiritual empowerment to do God's will (Matt. 4:1, 11), those who are entering into an intense period of prayer (Matt. 14:23), and those who are newly married (Deut. 24:5).

Chapter 98
A Deeper Walk of Faith

One of the conditions for safe, enjoyable boating is to make sure that the water is deep enough. If the water is too shallow, a person runs the risk of running aground and breaking out the bottom of their boat. Similarly, spiritual shallowness is not a good condition for any woman's personal life! How can you develop a deep walk with the Lord one that protects you from the shallowness of life? In Proverbs (2:1-9), we find these four provisions that help a person "walk with depth"

Saturate Your Life with the Word. Respond to the Word of God and know it inside and out. Have faith in God's inspiration of Scripture (2 Tim 3:16). If you doubt inspiration, you will doubt verse after verse, and the Bible will hold no constants for you.

Desire God's Word. Be open to what God is saying to you, and begin to desire what He has for you: "turning your ear to wisdom and applying your heart to understanding." Make reading God's Word a daily habit. Make it a priority.

People do what they want to do. All of us make choices and when we don't make time for God in our day, when we don't make time for the most important relationship in our life, when we don't make time to read His words to us, we are probably not making the best choices. Choose to do what is important, not only what is urgent.

The more you know of God's Word, the more you will fall in love with God's words and seek to live by them....

Develop a Prayer Life. Prayer is the way an alpha woman in Christ really get to know who God is. It is a time when God can speak to your heart.

Proverbs 2:3 challenges us to "call out for insight and cry aloud for understanding."

As a part of your prayer time each day:

- PRAISE God for who He is, the Creator and Sustainer of the whole universe who is interested in each of us who are in His family (Psalm 150, Matthew 10:30).
- THANK God for all He has done for you…for all He is doing for you ….and for all that He will do for you in the future (Philippians 4:6).
- CONFESS your sins. Tell God about the things you have done and said and thought for which you are sorry. He tells us in 1 John 1:9 that He is "faithful and righteous to forgive us our sins."
- PRAY for your family…and for friends or neighbors who have needs, physical or spiritual. Ask God to work in the heart of someone you hope will come to know Jesus as Savior. Pray for your government officials, for your minister and church officers, for missionaries and other Christian servants (Philippians 2:4).
- PRAY, too, for yourself. Ask for guidance for the day ahead. Ask God to help you do His will…and ask Him to arrange opportunities to serve Him throughout the day (Philippians 4:6).

Be Consistent in Your Walk. Prospectors often spend years searching for gold or silver. They are persistent and consistent. Make that your approach to God's Word. There are no overnight miracles when it comes to overcoming the shallowness of life. The race of life is not a sprint, but a marathon. If a woman will abide by these four principles, she will learn "the fear and the knowledge of God." If a woman will abide by these four principles, she will learn "the fear and the knowledge of God." That is a high-tide mark! Your boat will not run aground in shallow spiritual waters if you're truly know and have a deep reverential awe of God.

Chapter 99
Disabilities Friends with Special Needs

More than anything else disabled people need friends acquaintances, casual, close, or especially intimate. No matter what form of impairment the disabled person has, she needs friends who give unconditional love.

The faith, creativity, and commitment of friends helped a paralyzed man experience the healing power of Jesus. Four concerned friends took their paralyzed friend to see Jesus (Mark 2:1-12). After overcoming a seemingly unsurmountable hurdle, the friends laid the paralytic at the feet of Jesus. When Jesus healed the man, He took special note of the faith exhibited by the four friends.

The disabled person needs friends who give more comfort than advice. Friends should continue giving of self despite barriers architectural or attitudinal involving persons with disabilities in activities and in ministry. Integrate people with impairments with the able-bodied in worship. Evangelize disables friends. Look past the gizmos, gadgets, and electrical wizardry to get to know the individual as a person. Have the attitude, "If I don't reach out to this individual with the gospel and God's love, who will?"

Tender mercies, kindness, humility, meekness, and longsuffering are essential to friendship with a disabled person. Alpha women in Christ are also challenged to rise above all these obstacles and "put on charity" (Col. 3:12-14). Unconditional love overlooks physical or mental handicaps and focuses on the true person, a special object of God's care and concern. An intimate relationship with a disabled friend or family member can be a special way to discover what real love is all about.

Chapter 100
Evangelism: Women and the Great Commission

When Christ gave the Great Commission, He did not consider gender, just as gender is not a consideration when the Holy Spirit imparts spiritual gifts. God has chosen every believing woman to carry His message to her sphere of influence as she is filled and controlled by the Holy Spirit and anointed and equipped with His power (Acts 1:8). The mission of every alpha woman in Christ is to communicate to the world who Jesus is and to extend to all His offer of salvation and spiritual refuge. Jesus has commissioned all Alpha women in Christ to go to the most distant and remote points of the earth as well as to their neighbors next door to reach the lost with the gospel message of redemption and reconciliation. We are to make the Savior known

- through the spoken word (Rom. 10:14, 15),
- through good works (James 2:14-17).
- through the example of a new character (Matt. 5:16, 20).

The single woman, the wife, the mother, the grandmother, the widow are called to "go ye into all the world." "Going" does not necessarily mean leaving home and family, but it does mean making yourself totally available to serve wherever, whenever, and however He directs. The foremost manifestation of the Holy Spirit in an alpha woman in Christ's life is that she will be a witness of the Lord's life and commandments (Acts 1:8). She is to be ready at all times to speak His name, tell of His marvelous works, give a defense of the reason for our hope, and tell others about His sacrifice and the abundant life He provides now and for all eternity (1 Pet. 3:15).

The New Testament gives certain requirements for soul-winning. The first, of course, is a genuine experience of grace through a personal relationship with Jesus Christ (1 John 1:1-3). A love for Christ and for people is also essential (Ps. 126:6), as is a willingness to be used by the Holy Spirit in sharing the gospel (Acts 8:29). An effective soul-winner will determine to live a separated life (2 Cor. 6:17) since lifestyle testimony is also key ingredient. Creativity in using every opportunity for saying a word about Christ is also helpful (1 Pet. 3:15), as is a diligence in study of God's Word, which enables the alpha woman in Christ to explain more effectively the way of salvation (Ps. 51:13; 1 Pet. 2:2). All must be undergirded with specific and unceasing prayer (1 Thess. 5:17). Any woman willing to commit herself to this high and holy responsibility will indeed be rewarded (Dan. 12:3).

When unbelievers see those in the church generously giving their time, resources, and love to carry out the Great Commission, they are compelled to glorify the Father (Matt. 5:16).

Chapter 101
Divorce: Breaking Asunder

In interpreting the decree of Moses on divorce (Deut. 24:1), the followers of the Rabbi Shammai believed that divorce should be granted only because of infidelity; while the followers of Rabbi Hillel argued that Mosaic Law permitted divorce for virtually any reason. Jesus shocked His disciples by rejecting both sides of the rabbinic debate (Matt. 19:10). Rather than going immediately to the contested text (Deut. 24:1), Jesus referred back to the beginning of marriage (Matt. 19:4-6). Ultimately the answer to this problematic issue does not lie in legal codes, traditional practice, or human solutions but in God's creative design (Gen. 2:24). God never accommodates or compromises His principles, but He does redeem and restore any who seek His forgiveness.

Jesus' review of divorce ("to send away," meaning "to remove from the center of relationship" or "to break fellowship") can be understood only against the background of His view of permanent monogamy, one man and one woman together for a lifetime. The plan for permanence is clear in the one-flesh metaphor use by the Lord. Moses allowed divorce as a human device to protect ill-treated Hebrew women from unscrupulous men who sought to manipulate the betrothal process. The Pharisees toot the "permission" of the Law and turned it into a "command" that made human frailty a justification for circumventing God's divine plan and purpose.

Jesus did not teach that the innocent party must divorce the unfaithful one. The purpose of the "exception" clause in the Mosaic Law, which is repeated again Jesus' explanation, is not to encourage divorce. The binding commitment of marriage does not depend upon human wills or upon what any individual does or does not do but rather upon God's original design and purpose for marriage (Hos. 3:1-3).

God rejects divorce for these reasons:

1. Marriage is a divine institution the Lord used to teach His children about their relationship to Him (Gen. 1:27; Matt. 19:4).
2. Marriage is by express command of the Creator and carries His imprimatur (Matt. 19:4, 5)
3. Marriage brings two people together as one flesh, testifying to the permanence God planned for this most intimate union (Matt. 19:6).
4. Jesus points to the example of the first couple (Matt. 19:8).
5. Evil consequences are inevitable when separation comes (Matt. 19:9).

Divorce is never God's choice. Indeed, God hates divorce (Mal. 2:16). Furthermore, whenever divorce occurs for whatever reason, God desires to work redemptively when the person who has experienced this tragedy is repentant and desires reconciliation to God.

Chapter 102
Conflict: Resolving Disagreements

Conflict inevitable in personal relationships. It is humanly impossible to live in total harmony with others at all times. Jesus told His disciples how to settle dispute between believers (Matt. 18:15-20). Paul resolved his conflict with John Mark, which had developed between the first and second missionary journeys (Acts 15:36-41). John warned Christians not to hate each other (1 John 4:20, 21).

The Bible offers several steps to resolving conflict and settling disagreements among people:

1. Scripture admonishes the alpha woman in Christ to face the conflict acknowledge its existence and accept its impact. Christ advised His disciples to go immediately and directly to the person and discuss the grievance (Matt. 18:15). Others should be enlisted to mediate the conflict only if the conflict cannot be resolved one-to-one (Matt. 18:16, 17).

2. Scripture instructs the alpha woman in Christ to forgive the conflict to put the disagreement behind and move ahead in harmony once it has been resolved. Euodia and Syntyche were encouraged to replace their bitterness with gentleness and to live in peaceful harmony, rejoicing in the Lord (Phil. 4:2-7).

3. Scripture encourages the alpha woman in Christ to move beyond the conflict. Paul resolved his grudge against Mark and sought opportunities to minister with him (compare Acts 15:36-41 with 2 Tim. 4:9-11; Eccl. 1, Healing).

Jesus reminded the Pharisees of the greatest commandments to love the Lord and love your neighbor (Matt. 22:37-40). The desire of God is for His children to live in harmony. Alpha women in Christ are to resolve conflict with others by replacing discord with love. The emphasis is not punitive but redemptive (2 Cor. 2:5-11; 2 Thess. 3:14, 15).

Chapter 103
Remarriage: An Awesome Challenge

The question of remarriage is closely related to the matter of divorce. The Scripture lifts up permanent, monogamous union as the plan of the Creator (Matt. 19:4-6). To understand the strong language of Scripture concerning this matter, look at the whole of Scripture to see how God regards marriage. The marriage bond between husband and wife is the same kinship bond that exists between parents and children and between God and His creation (Gen. 2:24; Matt. 19:6).

Some argue that remarriage is never permissible (Mark 10:11, 12). Others note that the divorce teaching of Jesus includes an exception (Matt. 5:32; 19:9) and conclude that this implies permission to remarry. Still others suggest that the understood meaning of "divorce" in ancient law included freedom to remarry, suggesting that remarriage is forbidden only after an invalid divorce. Finally, there are those who deny that Jesus gives a justification for divorce in the modern sense, although they allow that remarriage is permissible if reconciliation with a divorced spouse is rendered impossible because of death or remarriage of the divorce spouse to another partner (1 Cor. 7:10, 11), or if the divorced spouse is a non-believer opposed to reconciliation (1 Cor. 7:15).

Despite these differences of biblical interpretation, some important conclusions can be drawn:

1. Once remarriage follows divorce, there is no turning back (Deut. 24:1-4), and the tearing apart of a marriage is painful, leaving its scars on all who are touched by the tragedy.
2. God sees the one-flesh relationship as permanent and binding because it is the picture He has chosen to portray His relationship to His children, and thus He guards the home with great zeal (Mal. 2:16).

3. Jesus gives no divine directive nor even acceptable excuses for breaking this holy covenant but rather observes that the hardness of the human heart makes such tragedy a reality in this sinful world (Matt. 19:8).

4. The role of the church and of alpha women in Christ must always be redemptive. With God, forgiveness is as if it never happened. No sin or tragedy is beyond God's forgiveness.

After seeking and receiving God's forgiveness, a woman who remarries has a new understanding of God's incredible grace. She must then seek anew an understanding of God's plan for marriage (Gen. 2:24), commit herself wholeheartedly to pursuing His plan, and consider her vows of marriage binding before the Lord (Matt. 19:5, 6).

Chapter 104
Engagement: A Step in Commitment

Engagement or betrothal, in Jewish culture, was a formal bond between a man and a woman, almost as binding as marriage itself, yet without physical intimacy. According to the Law of Moses, the penalty for carelessly breaking this commitment through fornication, adultery, incest, or rape was death by stoning (Deut. 22:23-30). Under some circumstances, the engagement could be broken by a bill of divorcement.

The time period for an engagement was usually about a year. Mary and Joseph were betrothed or engaged but did not live together during that engagement period. Joseph is called Mary's "husband" (Matt. 1:19), although the relationship was still physically celibate.

In modern culture, engagement is considered a couple's promise of intent for uniting in marriage, although it is not binding. In fact, engagement is seen as the time of deepening intimacy in which a couple has the freedom to make sure that marriage is the step they ought to take. Becoming engaged is the first step toward the joining to two lives, the blending of two personalities and families, replete with the potential of many generations to come.

Chapter 105
Renewal: Returning to the Lord

The corruption of the church seems to be increasing. The pattern found in Scripture and throughout church history, however, is this: Again and again God's people have done what is right in their own eyes (Judg. 21:25), and God must call them back to obedience. The Law is given and the prophets are sent. The message of John the Baptist, then Jesus, is delivered to the lost sheep of Israel: "Repent ye: for the kingdom of heaven is at hand" (Matt. 3:2). Admonitions against apostasy, disunity, and immorality fill the New Testament epistles. The prophet Hosea's longsuffering love for Gomer is a parable of the price God will pay to woo His people back to Him (Hos. 3:1-5).

One of the key roles of Christ today is to sanctify and cleanse the church (Eph. 5:25-27). Scripture strongly condemns religious leaders who lead others astray (Matt. 23:24, 27, 33). The biblical view of the church is not of a club that we can easily leave when problems arise (1 Cor. 12:21). Instead, we must labor as Paul did (1 Cor. 11:1).

Chapter 106
Sacrifice: Living Here Is My Life

A sacrifice is an offering rendered acceptable to God. To live sacrificially is to offer your entire life to God. Such a sacrifice is acceptable to God only because of Christ's work in you; He is the final and complete Sacrifice for the atonement of sin (Heb. 7:26, 27).

Micah knew lavish offerings were not acceptable to God (Mic. 6:6-8). David and Isaiah knew acceptability with God was "a contrite heart" (Ps. 51:17; Is. 66:2). Paul described this transaction as a "living sacrifice" (Rom. 12:1). Although you can never match Christ's sacrificial death and indeed, are not asked to do so yourself, giving is to be complete and whole-hearted. Being a living sacrifice means obeying the greatest commandments: giving God all your love, will, reason, and body (Mark 12:29-31), borne out in practical, daily service to others (Matt. 25:34-40). No expression of love, however costly, matches the price paid by Christ. The forgiven woman poured out expensive, fragrant oil at anoint Jesus' feet, but her gift also involved the recognition of her past and the risk of disclosure of her sin. Her example of sacrificial giving did not go unnoticed (Luke 7:46-50).

Chapter 107
Marriage: Principles from God

Marriage is the oldest relationship in the world, established by a sovereign Creator in the Garden of Eden. In that beautiful, perfect setting, God organized the home by assigning roles and defining responsibilities to Adam and Eve.

Adam was to be the provider ("to dress" the garden), the protector ("and keep" the garden), and the leader ("the Lord God commanded the man..."). His assigned occupation was to care for the garden and those in it (Gen. 2:15-17). This demanded the type of servant leadership emulated by Jesus (Eph. 5:21-33). Certainly there is no room for abuse or tyranny directed to a wife on the part of her husband, nor is there the option of a wife's willful disregard for her husband's leadership.

The woman's responsibilities were several: She was to be "help meet" (Gen. 2:18), a comforter (Gen. 24:67), and an encourager (Prov. 31:12, 26). Eve was Adam's partner for carrying out God's purpose to multiply and replenish the earth (Gen. 1:28). She was to be his closest earthly companion, relieving his loneliness (Gen. 2:18).

When sin entered the world, chaos followed. God's plan did not change, but it was distorted by the sinful choices of Adam and Eve and their descendants. God let Adam and Eve choose to sin, but He did not let choose to sin's consequences. Fear emerged; they were afraid to face God because of their disobedience (Gen. 3:10). They were cast out of their idyllic home with this foretelling: Adam's work would become difficult because he would have to contend with thorns and thistles (Gen. 3:17, 18), and Eve would suffer pain in childbirth (Gen. 3:16). Adam and Eve and their posterity would have spiritual warfare until the end of time.

Despite the failure of Adam and Eve, God's principles for marriage have remained the same according to their God-defined roles, husbands are to use their God-given authority to provide, to protect, and to love (Gen. 2:15-17;

Eph. 5:25), and wives are to help their husbands and submit to their God-directed leadership (Gen. 2:18; Eph. 5:23, 24). Husbands and wives can ignore God's program for the home, but when a spiritual principle is violated, division is the result. They can seek to redefine God's plan according to their own desires and circumstances, but ultimately human wisdom cannot compete with the all-wise God. There can be no unity, no contentment, and no peace only a house divided in a marriage that defies God's principles. Husbands and wives are challenged to spend time, energy, and creativity looking for ways to conform to servant leadership and Christ like submission.

Chapter 108
Adultery: Unfaithfulness in Marriage

A theme running throughout Scripture is God's intent for husbands and wives to be faithful to each other. Fidelity in marriage is God's plan for His kingdom and God's purpose for His children. Adultery when a husband or wife willfully engages in sexual intercourse with someone other than the marriage partner is prohibited (Ex. 20:14; Deut. 5:18). Many Old Testament regulations prescribed severe punishment for adultery (Lev. 20:10; Deut. 22:22). In the New Testament, Jesus condemned adultery (Mark 10:11, 12; Luke 16:18), and Paul denounced it as one of the "works of the flesh" (Gal. 5:19).

Adulterers can receive God's forgiveness (John 8:3-11) from extramarital sexual infidelity, which is an act of unfaithfulness. Believers are to practice faithfulness to God and in their personal relationships. A spouse who is able to forgive adulterous behavior on the part of a mate is encouraged to remain within a marriage. At the same time, in Scripture, adultery is regarded as such a severe breach of trust and fidelity that it is noted as permissible grounds for divorce (Matt. 5:32).

Jesus taught that adultery begins in the heart (Matt. 5:27, 28; 19:18, 19) and is rooted in lust. Many a marriage has suffered greatly because of emotional adultery, which Jesus taught was just as serious as sexual immorality. In part, adultery was dealt with so harshly in Scripture because it distorts one of God's illustrations about Himself and His intentions toward His creation. God wants to use the faithfulness between husband and wife to illustrate His faithfulness to His people. For this reason, adultery is likened to idolatry in the Old Testament. To commit adultery is to distort the very relationship God wants with those whom He loves.

Chapter 109
Marriage: A Metaphor of Union with God

Throughout Scripture the marriage union is a metaphor or picture of the relationship between God and His people in the Old Testament, Israel is pictured as the wife of Yahweh. When Israel became unfaithful and worshiped other gods, she was described as a harlot (Jer. 3:1; Ezek. 23). Her spiritual adultery became so despicable in God's sight that He issued a writing of divorcement (Jer. 3:8). Actually, this was a separation, as God in His great love for His chosen people could not bear to cut off Israel without a promise of renewal (Hos. 2:14-20; 5:15).

In the Epistles and in Revelation, the church is described as the Bride of Christ. The experience of obtaining a bride similar for both Adam and Christ, Adam was put to sleep; Christ was laid in a tomb. When Christ came to earth in human form, He left His Father. When He began His earthly ministry and ultimately died on the Cross, He left His mother. This was for the purpose of cleaving to the object of His love, His people. As He is received into the heart of each sinner, they become one flesh (Gen. 2:24; 1 Cor. 6:15).

The whole focus and course of a life is changed both by marriage and a personal experience with Jesus Christ. Marriage (1 Cor. 7:3) and becoming a child of God (Mark 8:34; 1 Cor. 6:20; 7:23) both demand death to self and accountability to God and to others. A wife or husband cannot be faithful to more than one partner, as a Christian cannot serve any other God (Matt. 6:24). Alpha woman in Christ should have no hesitation in giving themselves in totality to God because of the high price He paid for us (1 Pet. 1:18, 19). God has given all He has to give; He now expects our all in response (Rom. 12:1, 2).

In marriage, two hearts are grafted together, making them dependent on one another for life. This is depicted in John 15, with Jesus as the vine and believers as the branches. Through the infilling of the Holy Spirit and His control in the life of both partners, this picture of marriage and the parallel relationship of Christ and His Bride come into focus. The Holy Spirit fills and fulfills both.

Chapter 110
Motherhood: Mothers and Daughters

Mothers often fail to savor the precious, fleeting, moments with their daughters. In rushing through life, they sometimes take time only for the high spots, while the small, daily experiences that give life its character and the most delicious and meaningful moments are all but lost in the shuffle. The lasting and eternal are engulfed in triviality.

There is no better opportunity to enjoy life's small, mundane responsibilities than to invest time and energy in lifestyles teaching of you daughter giving her instruction on how to care for younger children, to fix family meals, to study the art and method of homemaking, even teaching her to set a table with care and creativity (Titus 2:3-5). Sensing pleasure and significance in caring for the simple of the family is caught as well as taught (2 Cor. 3:2, 3) so that irksome, bothersome, and irritating chores become meaningful, delightful, and rewarding opportunities for service.

There are many practical ways of spending time together without making elaborate plans. In the biblical story of Mary and Martha, Martha was not rebuked by the Lord for setting the table, cooking, sweeping the floor, or decorating the house. She was not doing anything wrong, but her priorities were not right at that time. Busy with good things, she missed her opportunity for the best thing (Luke 10:38-42). Many mothers today are busy with good things, but miss the opportunity for the best thing, investing time in a daughter (Ps. 127:3-5).

Childhood cannot be used over again for another set of memories (Deut. 6:10-25). Therefore, the spending of time is an irrevocable act that cannot be used again (Eph. 5:15-17). No day or even hour can be recaptured. What greater delight than to work side by side with your daughters, mentoring, and modeling and sharing.

Chapter 111
Clothing: Garments in Bible Times

The Bible teaches that alpha women in Christ are not to fret over what they are going to wear (Matt. 6:25-30), they are not to judge others by what they wear, nor are they to show favor based upon how well someone is dressed (James 2:2-4). They are to be generous in clothing the poor (Matt. 25:36, 44). Embroidered cloth, leather sandals, and fine linen were typical clothing (Is. 3:18-23; Ezek. 16:9-13). Gold and silver jewelry included bracelets, necklaces, earrings, crowns, and even nose rings often encrusted with jewels.

Both men and women in Bible times wore tunics as their primary garments. These were loose-fitting, dress-like garments with sleeves to the mid-forearm. They were tucked at the waist, sometimes by a money pocket, a belt, or more commonly, by a sash. Women's tunics were usually decorated with embroidery. A man was forbidden by the Law to wear a woman's garment, and vice versa (Deut. 22:5).

Fabrics mentioned in Scripture include goat and camel hair (Matt. 3:4), leather, linen (Lev.16:4; Ezek. 16:10; Rev. 18:12; 19:14), and wool (Job. 31:20). In Bible times, the texture of a garment was a sign of weather. Rough-textured garments were worn by the poor. Since dyes were expensive, garments generally were in the natural colors. The Israelites, however, did weave colored threads including gold thread into the fabric of special garment (Ex. 39:3).

Head coverings included veils that were used to hide a woman's beauty from strangers until she was united with her husband in marriage. Once married, an Israelite woman was not bound to wear a veil, but she generally continued to cover her face in the presence of strangers (Gen. 24:65). High priests covered their heads in the temple, and women also were admonished to cover their heads in worship services of the first-century church (1 Cor. 11:5, 6).

Footwear, especially sandals, provided protection from scorching sands and rocky paths but were not worn inside homes. Hosts showed kindness to their guests by removing their shoes at the home's entrance and washing their feet (Luke 7:44; John 13:5). Shoes were also moved in the temple and on "holy ground" and were not worn during times of mourning. Footwear also has symbolic meaning in the Scriptures. Boaz sealed his marriage contract with Ruth using a shoe (Ruth 4:7-10). To lift up your shoe to show its sole or heel to another person was considered an insult (Ps. 41:9).

Chapter 112
Prayer: Rooted in God's Promises

Prayer is one way in which the believer claims the promises of God. Through prayer God reveals His character and His belongings. His precious promises are apparent to believers as they pray (2Pet. 1:2-4). God makes several promises to His children who are committed to prayer. First and foremost, He promises a response. God promises to hear and to answer the prayer of every sinner who seeks forgiveness and to act on the request of every believer who asks in faith. Jesus told His disciples that the Father would do anything asked in His name (John 14:13, 14).

To the alpha woman in Christ, God's answer at first may be unclear or different from the answer you expected or desired, or the answer may be delayed. God's answers include "yes," "no," and "wait." Alpha women in Christ must recognize in praying that sometimes you ask the Lord to do things that are not for your good, the good of others, or the ultimate fulfillment of God's plan. You see life from a limited, finite viewpoint; He alone can see the beginning and ending of all things. The Lord alone knows how your prayer requests fit into His purpose which is both for your good and the good of all other believers.

Second, God promises His presence through prayer. When alpha women in Christ are called by name, she should respond with attention. When you call God by name, He gives you His ear. From the time of salvation, an alpha woman in Christ is promised the presence of the Holy Spirit as Helper, Tutor, and Guide (Acts 2:33). The Holy Spirit through His presence fulfills the promises of God to and in believers.

Third, God promises His wisdom as alpha women in Christ pray. Often during a time of crisis, a believer does not know how to pray. At other times a believer may not know what to pray (Jude 20). God promises to answer the sincere intent of the heart, even if you cannot find the right words. When an alpha woman prays in faith, God does even more than He is asked (Jer. 33:3). He answers us liberally, abundantly, and generously.

Chapter 113
Widowhood: Trusting God to Provide

God sometimes asks questions that reveal truths otherwise unseen. To the penniless widow with two sons for whom to care, God asked what she had in the house. Though the widow's response was that she had "not anything in the house, save a pot of oil" (2 Kin. 4:2), she was touched by the living God at this turning point in her life. Like the widow, when all else is gone, God's children always have the oil of His Spirit within (1 Cor. 3:16, 17). It is to be used only as He personally directs (1 Cor. 6:19, 20).

When Elisha requested the widow to act in order to meet her needs, he undoubtedly rekindled hope in her heart (2 Kin. 4:3). God never leaves His children without resources for all circumstances. The answer may not be what was expected, but by listening to His heart the believing woman will come to understand that He is providing for her good and His glory (Jer. 29:11; Phil. 4:19).

Widows without means of support became the responsibility for the people as a whole, just as the Levites, strangers, and orphans (Deut. 14:29). This concept of care for widows was readily embraced by the early church. Paul gave very specific advice to Timothy about the definition and care of widows (1 Tim. 5:3-16).

Widows face unending challenges. By relying on God's character and determining to become more like Him, there are forever changed. The widow to whom God sent Elisha never hesitated or questioned the prophet's unusual request. She listened intently (2 Kin. 4:5). She remembered his instructions. And she immediately "went from him" into active work she knew to be God's plan for her. She had all the resources she would ever need God's presence within (Phil. 4:13). Widows and all women have that same power available as they face the complexities of an ever-changing world.

Everyone in the church is called to care for widows both materially and spiritually (Acts 6:1). The church should undergird and provide support for those who have no means of support and should give freely of time and life to widows. As part of giving to widows, an active effort should be made to include them in all activities of the church and to invite them to be a part of celebrations within the church family.

Chapter 114
Attributes of God: He Is Omnipresent

The active presence of God, both in places and in relationships, is one of the chief presuppositions running through Scripture. There is no place without God, no place beyond Him (2 Chr. 6:18), and He is everywhere simultaneously (Eph. 4:6). Yet God is not bound by, nor dependent upon, any place or anyone (Jer. 23:23, 24).

God's universal presence encompasses all space extending to every geographical location (Ps. 33:18; 34:15; 121:1-8), creation (Ps. 104), and all human affairs (Is. 40:21-23). This in no way suggests that He is immersed in His creation, as pantheism suggests. God is always distinct from His creation because He, as the Creator, brought all into existence (Gen. 1:31). His relational presence is experienced only by believers. He indwells His children (1 Cor. 6:19, 20). In taking up residence, He establishes ownership, provision, love, workmanship, guidance, teaching, and personal friendship (Ps. 139).

Jesus reveals what God's presence is like. In a created universe filled with energy and wonder, God's passion was and is to have a relationship with every man and woman (John 1:1-18). God does not come and go in our lives rather, we live and move and have our being in Him (Acts 17:27, 28; Phil. 1:6).

Chapter 115
Paganism: Following False God's

Solomon was a man of great God-given wisdom; yet his heart was turned away from the Lord by His foreign wives (1 Kin. 11:1-8). Even though God had appeared to Solomon twice, warning him of the danger of following false gods, ultimately Solomon did not listen and chose to follow his own sinful heart instead of God.

Likewise, Israel's King Ahab was influenced by his Sidonian wife, Jezebel, to worship Baal demanded the slaying of all the prophets of the Lord God of Israel, and on one occasion she demanded the slaying of all the prophets of the Lord she could find (1 Kin. 18:4). Her threats upon the life of Elijah, because he had executed the prophets of Baal, sent the prophet into hiding and deep depression (1 Kin. 19:1-4).

Not only foreign women, but the women of Israel themselves, influenced God's people to embrace pagan gods (Jer. 7:16-18; Ezek. 8:14). With the full permission of their husbands, the women of Israel and Judah baked cakes to offer to the queen of heaven; they also burned incense and poured out drink offerings to her. These men and women were totally unrepentant when confronted with their sin. Therefore, God pronounced judgment upon them through Jeremiah (Jer. 44:15-29).

In recent times, a renewed interest in paganism has arisen among many women. Focus has been placed upon such ancient goddesses as Gaia, the earth goddess, and Sophia, the goddess of wisdom. Some women's organizations, even within the church, are introducing women to goddesses and pagan elements of worship and theology.

Alpha women in Christ must guard their hearts and minds against these influences. The power of their persuasion must be used to turn the hearts of men, women, and children not away from but toward the one true God as revealed in Jesus Christ.

Chapter 116
Abortion: Defending the Innocent

Although the Bible does not specifically address the subject of abortion, Scripture clearly regards the unborn child as fully human life. This life is to be protected in the same way that God calls us to defend the lives of all innocent human beings. Jesus affirmed the value of unborn life in the womb through His Incarnation coming as a baby rather than arriving on earth as an adult (Matt. 1:20, 21, 25). Other passages of Scripture also affirm the extensions of the sanctity of life to the unborn. The psalmist speaks of God's care for the baby while still in the womb (Ps. 139:13-16), and the Mosaic Law punished violence done to the unborn the same as violence done to a full-grown adult (Ex. 21:22-25).

The existence of a person is established at conception. God had plans for you before you were born (Jer. 1:4, 5), and He tells you He has been your God since before your birth (Ps. 22:10). John the Baptist "leaped" while in the womb of his mother Elizabeth as she acknowledged the coming of the Messiah (Luke 1:41-45). These verses all speak of the unborn child as an actual human being, not a mere potential that will become a human being at birth.

The unborn child is to be protected because the child is a life (Ex. 21:22-25); God does get angry over the killing of unborn children (Amos 1:13). An unintended pregnancy can be difficult for a woman and her family, but God wants both the woman and her unborn child to be protected and cherished. However, a woman who has had an abortion, for whatever reason, needs to know that Jesus still loves her stands ready to forgive her just as He freely forgave women who erred against His law in other ways (John 8:1-11).

Chapter 117
Motherhood: A Noble Ministry

A mother is one who bears and/or rears children. References to motherhood are found throughout Scripture: conception (Gen. 4:1), pregnancy (Luke 1:24), childbirth (Is. 66:7-9), breastfeeding (1 Sam. 1:23). Mothers were to be respected and obeyed (Ex. 20:12). More than a job or responsibility, mothering is ministry. Most assuredly it takes work! It means sacrifice. Children do not come off an assembly line, nor are they the byproduct of an impersonal biological process; they are to be lovingly nurtured by their mothers (2 Tim. 1:3-5). Mothers divide time among their children but multiply their love for all their children. To this they add the care of the home, often subtracting many extras in order to do so.

When Isaiah the prophet searched for an illustration of God's constant love for His people, the best example he could find was a new baby's mother (Is. 49:15). Mothers have enduring love that even the most trying circumstances or rebellious child cannot dim. As a mother lets go of her own life for the sake of her child, she is reminded of the depth and height and breadth of God's lover of her, and in a unique way she experiences the true joy of motherhood. This is a truth that will transform any suffering or sacrifice into reward and joy (1 John 3:16).

There are caring mothers in the Bible: Hagar, wandering in the wilderness, wept of her child, and God responded to the cry of her heart by revealing a well of water nearby to quench the thirst of her and her child (Gen. 21:16, 19). Jochebed defied Pharaoh in order to save the life of her son (Ex. 2:1-8). The mother who appealed to Solomon was willing to let another woman enjoy her child rather than see the child murdered (1 Kin. 3:26). The mother from Shunem loved her child so devotedly that she made the difficult journey to find the prophet and inspired him to come and seek life for her child (2 Kin. 4:22-35). Hannah was devoted to her son, yet willingly offered him to the Lord (1

Sam. 1:27, 28). On the other hand, there are wicked mothers such as Athaliah, the idolatrous mother of King Ahaziah, who guided her son into devotion to evil (2 Kin. 8:26, 27).

God has a plan mothers (Ex. 2:1-10). The high calling is an all-consuming task (Deut. 6:6, 7): in the morning, you can read God's Word to your child; at mealtime you are to give attention to meeting physical needs; as you are outside, you can teach your child about the beauty of creation; at bedtime you can pray for your child give assurance. The reward is worth the effort (Prov. 31:28). Godly mothers are the nation's greatest treasure, the Lord's best helpers, and the most blessed among women.

Chapter 118
Prisoners: Reaching Beyond Bars

Prisoners are those accused and convicted, whether justly or unjustly, of criminal activity. Joseph was imprisoned in Egypt (Gen. 39:20). The prophet Jeremiah had perhaps the worst experience as he was confined to a muddy cistern or underground dungeon (Jer. 37:16). John the Baptist was murdered while in prison (Matt. 14:3-12).

Paul, who was thrown in jail for his faith, often called himself a prisoner of Jesus Christ (Acts 16:23, 24). The apostle was delivered from spiritual imprisonment on accepting Christ as his Savior; he then submitted himself to physical imprisonment that the Word of God might move forward.

Causes for imprisonment ranged from offending the king (Gen. 40:1-3) or differing with his policies (2 Chr. 16:10) to an accusation of treason (Jer. 37:11-15). Treatment of prisoners was harsh (Judg. 16:21; Jer. 29:26). Prison is Satan's domain over which he has ruled through the ages. Yet the Light dispels darkness. Those who suffer for the gospel's sake will be delivered (Ps. 146:7). Believers are reminded to give love and support to those under persecution because of their work for Christ and to share the gospel with all prisoners (Acts 16:25).

Individuals who reach out to prisoners in loving compassion demonstrate the spirit of Christ, for His own description of His messianic task from the prophet Isaiah (61:1-3) included the opening of the prison (Matt. 25:34-44; Luke 4:18-21). Salvation opened the spiritual prison, but our Lord also showed His compassion for those languishing in an earthly prison. They, too, need the gospel and loving concern.

Chapter 119
Grief: Sorrow of Soul

Sorrow of soul, such as the disciples experienced at the imminent death of Jesus, is a very real thing (Luke 22:45). God expects us to grieve when we are brokenhearted (John 11:19, 31-35). Unexpressed grief often brings complex emotional and physical illness. Release from grief and inner happiness comes only when you offer your unique circumstances to God so that He can cause them to bear fruit on your behalf (John 7:37, 38). As Jesus used the words of the prophet Isaiah to describe Himself and His messianic role, He included the replacement of the signs of sorrow ashes, mourning, or the spirit of heaviness with the marks of victory beauty, joy, and the garment of praise (Is. 61:1-3; Luke 4:18-21).

Jesus identifies with your broken hearted because He is "a man of sorrows, and acquainted with grief" (Is. 53:3). He understands when you hurt (Is. 53:4).

Jesus wept (John 11:35) and taught His children by example at the Cross to express openly feelings of protest, sadness, anxieties, and fears (Matt. 26:39; 27:46).

For women, grief is not confined to the death of a loved one. It also includes sorrow at the tearing apart of anything that they have thought to be secure, such as a marriage, possessions, job, health, relationships, or finances. Believers must remember that grief is not forever. It is healed through a deliberate, personal, lived-out experience of the unfailing grace of God (2 Cor. 12:9).

Chapter 120
Culture: The Judeo-Christian Heritage

The culture of a people includes its language, customs, laws, mores, traditions, music, and art, symbols, artifacts; everything that points toward the best of a group of people and those things which the group desires to pass on to future generations. The Bible may very well be considered the handbook for Judeo-Christian culture since it clearly defines the essence of what it means to be God's people (Is. 51:16).

The Bible clearly states that the culture of God's people is to have these hallmarks:

- To live in obedience to the Law of faith. To follow God's commands is to be in position to receive God's blessings; to disobey God's laws is to experience God's wrath (Ex. 15:26; Deut. 28:1-14).
- To have a heart for the one true and living God plus a heart for your neighbor. The Law's purpose is to reveal a heart for God and for others (Matt. 22:37-40).
- To maintain family alliances. God's people dwell in a community that has a family orientation. Inheritances are to be kept within a tribe (Deut. 32:6-9).

God's people "The Women in Christ" are strongly warned against diluting their culture through intermarriage with nonbelievers (2 Cor. 6:14-16) and endangering their culture through situations making them vulnerable to captivity and slavery (Deut. 7:2-5). Conversely, God's people are admonished to spread their culture to others (Acts 10:34-43) and to be a moral light to the nations (Acts 13:47). Women in the history of God's people held a unique responsibility for the transmission of culture within the family context. Religious descent among the Hebrews is matrilineal: If the mother is Jewish, then so is the child. Women are also responsible for preparing the most important cultural celebration: the Shabbat or Sabbath feast.

Chapter 121
Aging: The Passing of Years

The Bible offers repeated assurances that the process we call aging is completely secure in God's hand. Looks, health, and circumstances change with time and often in ways we would not desire. Many cope the stress of aging by trying to cling to outward beauty, youthful strength, or vocational achievement. Yet, only when we an alpha woman in Christ realize that God has made each of us and, in accordance with His plan, carries us through the changing seasons of life, do we come to peace with the inevitability of getting older.

Just as each season of nature has its beauty and purpose by God's design, so there is no season of life in which the alpha woman in Christ should despair of living. Though opportunities and abilities may decline with age, each day of life that God gives is purposefully ordained according to His perfect wisdom. God's plan includes people of every age. Miriam was a young girl when she stood by a river and watched her baby brother, Moses. Many years later, she helped her brother lead God's people across another body of water to freedom. Mary was teenager when Gabriel announced her motherhood and middle-aged when she witnessed His Crucifixion and Resurrection, and the sending of the Holy Spirit to the early church. Sarah was well past menopause when she gave birth to her son, Isaac. Those who live each day for Christ will bear fruit not only in youth but in old age as well (Ps. 92:12).

Chapter 122
Attributes of God: He Is Omniscient

God knows everything from eternity past to eternity future simultaneously. He learns from no one, is never surprised, and never forgets (Is. 46:9, 10). God knows His creation completely. He names the stars (Ps. 147:4, 5), places the clouds (Job 37:16), tracks activity in the oceans (Job 38:16), clothes the fields (Matt. 6:28), and is aware of every creature and its activities at all times (Matt. 10:29).

God knows each alpha woman in Christ fully (Ps. 33:15), her pass (Rev. 2:2, 3), where she goes, what she does, thinks, says (Ps. 33:13-15), and even her motivations (1 Sam 16:7).

The comforting news is that God knows and loves you anyway (Ps. 103:14). He knows the number of hairs on your head (Matt. 10:30), your needs (Matt. 6:8), your feelings (Is. 40:28, 29), and your future (John 14:2, 3). You can take comfort in these words in Scripture, "O Lord God, thou knowest" (Ezek. 37:3).

Chapter 123
Suffering: Experiencing God's Goodness in the Midst

God's goodness is nowhere more apparent than in the midst of suffering. His history of providential care and deliverance for His people remains a constant reminder in every generation that He is to carry us through every adversity and trial. His presence is sufficient to banish fear. His power is enough to deliver from despair. His ultimate purpose is always for our good (Rom. 8:28).

Much of our suffering as alpha women in Christ is rooted either in circumstances beyond our control, or in relationships. Everyone is affected by circumstances that bring suffering. Mary Magdalene, for example, had been possessed of demons. She testified to the suffering of body and mind she endured before meeting Jesus. The outpouring of devotion that she showed in following Jesus to the Cross (Mark 15:40, 47), as well as the unutterable joy she displayed to Jesus at the Garden after His resurrection (John 20:1, 11-18), left little doubt that she had known at a very deep level a response of love from our Lord that had liberated her from the demon possession she had previously suffered. In the light of His love, she experienced status, acceptance, and peace.

The Scripture have a number of stories of suffering that are rooted in a woman's relationships: mother, wife, sister, daughter, friend. One example is Mary, the mother of Jesus. As a result of her openness and obedience to God, she exposed herself to the suffering that was to manifest itself in various ways: She endangered her engagement to Joseph (Matt. 1:18-25); she filed into exile once Jesus was born in order to safeguard His life (Matt. 2:14-15); she suffered the rejection of Jesus as He moved out of the exclusiveness of His family to the inclusiveness of the kingdom of God (Mark 3:31-35); and finally, she suffered the agonies of watching her Son's cruel death on Calvary. As with other biblical motifs, suffering, however, does not have the final word; for with the Resurrection of the Lord, the arrows that pierced Mary's soul were turned to the joy that every alpha woman in Christ will experience at the Lord's return.

In the story of the Shunamite mother and her son is an insight into the profound suffering that comes peculiarly to mothers who experience the death of a dearly loved child (2 Kin. 4:8-37). Pathos and tragedy combine in the growing relationship between a family from Shunem and Elisha the prophet. Elisha received hospitality from a wealthy woman from Shunem. Her bareness obviously had not made her bitter because she was profoundly hospitable. As a result of her hospitality to Elisha, she was blessed with a son. What greater joy could a woman know that the blessing of a child, and yet what greater pain could she endure that to lose this through death. As with many biblical presentations of suffering, the pain is not belittled, but the promise of life broke through in her faith and obedience, which led to her son being raised to life.

Chapter 124
Employment: Relationships in the Workplace and at Home

An alpha woman in Christ who is employed outside her home faces numerous decisions on a daily basis about how to juggle various obligations and priorities. As an alpha woman in Christ evaluates her priorities and decisions, these guidelines may be helpful:

- Careers are usually based on contracts that are temporary; family relationships are covenants with spiritual commitment and are eternal. Employees and employers come and go, but a mother's children are hers for the rest of her life.
- Careers provide only part of a woman's identity. Ultimately, a woman is not what she does but who she is, which is largely determined by her relationships to God and to others.

When the inevitable feelings of guilt come, as the result of less than perfect choices, these principles of Scripture offer comfort: God created you and gave you the gifts and talents you choose to use in your career (Matt. 25:14-29). God's criterion for success is faithfulness with what you have been given to the task He has assigned (1 Cor. 4:2). You, as well as others, may expect perfection. Perfection is never possible, of course, but faithfulness is. God honors your efforts and intentions. He knows your weaknesses as well as your strengths. Neither your family members nor your colleagues in the workplace see the big picture of your life. God does. Conversely, he alone knows the way to meet all of the needs of those with whom you live or work.

An alpha woman in Christ who is employed must acknowledge that she is obligated in certain ways to her employer, regardless of their spiritual state.

For example, she owes her employer hard work (Prov. 10:4, 26; 15:19). An alpha woman in Christ should always give a full day's work and never take advantage of employers by cheating them out of time and work that is owed to them (Eccl. 9:10; 2 Tim. 2:15). She must be careful not to steal from her employer, doing everything she can to conserve their resources both time and material assets (Prov. 1:19). She owes her employer loyalty. An alpha woman in Christ should not be found slandering or gossiping about her employer (Titus 2:3).

Just as a woman must be willing to give an employer what is rightfully belonging to the employer, she must also give to God what is God's. For example, we do not owe our employer dishonesty of any sort, even if that employer should demand such (Prov. 2:12-15; 20:17). God requires a life of integrity and honesty, and an employer has no right to ask an employee to lie or deceive in any way.

An alpha woman in Christ does not owe her employer participation in any activity that is dishonorable (1 Cor. 10:31). That includes social occasions marked by lewd conversation or sinful behavior. No employer has a right to require an employee to take part in sexually or morally compromising situations in order to keep a job. Also, while an alpha woman in Christ owes her employer an honest day's work, she does not owe all her energy and time. She not only owes time and resources to God, but also God expects a balanced lifestyle with family and home priorities firmly established according to His divine order.

Chapter 125
Ecological Concerns: Our Habitats for Life

The Lord God created the earth to be a habitat for life (Is. 45:18). He blessed the earth and put it under our care (Gen. 1:26). But something went terribly wrong with this scenario when Adam and Eve rebelled against their Creator. To this day the earth is still groaning under the curse of our sinfulness (Rom. 8:19-25).

Jesus Christ came to redeem His creation from sin. The earth will share in that redemption when, at the end of history, He comes, freeing both the earth and its inhabitants from sin. The Bible speaks of an environmental restoration of global magnitude: a recreated earth (Rev. 21:1). Until that time, we have a responsibility to God to be good stewards of the earth He entrusted to us. We cannot exploit the earth's resources in greed and technological ambition. Nor must we care for the environment more than we care for people. In our attempt to protect the environment, we cannot forget that God created the earth in order to sustain the traffic of life upon it (Ps. 24:1).

While we must take our stewardship responsibilities seriously, we must also keep in mind that in the ultimate sense only Jesus Christ can restore the perfect balance between a new earth and a new humanity. Until that time, alpha woman in Christ are challenged to be wise stewards of God's good creation to be fruitful, multiply, and fill the earth even as we subdue it and take dominion over it (Gen. 1:28).

Chapter 126
The Virgin Birth: A Miracle of the Spirit

A virgin is one who has not engaged in sexual intercourse. The virgin birth describes the birth of the Savior, who was conceived in the womb of the young virgin. Mary through the miraculous work of the Holy Spirit and without the presence of an earthly father. God chose this mystery, which is beyond human understanding, to bring His Son into the world (Matt. 1:18; Luke 1:34, 35).

Belief in the virgin birth is foundational to the Christian faith because this affirms and guarantees the perfect union of the human and divine in Jesus, the God-Man (Is. 9:6, 7); this identifies Jesus as the "New Adam" (Rom. 5:14, 15); this enables Jesus in His sinless nature as the Son of God and His perfect obedience as the Son of Man to meet the requirements for redemption (Heb. 2:17; 1 John 2:1, 2; 4:9, 10). Being misunderstood is always painful, particularly when all the circumstantial evidence stacks up against you. Young, unmarried, and pregnant in a society that highly valued sexual purity and virginity, Mary surely was among the most misunderstood of women.

Mary's response to the angel's announcement to her must be seen in light of this tremendous high personal cost (Luke 1:38). She made a monumental declaration of faith. God asked Mary to bear the shame of pregnancy out of wedlock with only the knowledge of the truth as her strength the truth that she was in fact a virgin despite all appearances. Mary accepted God's Word that by His power alone the Holy Child would be planted inside her body, receiving Him in faith and giving witness to His presence.

Chapter 127
Attributes of God: His Is Holy

God is not among many; His is the One and Only (Is. 40:25). The word "holy" means "unique, set apart, unlike all others." God's holiness is a powerful study of contrasts. The threefold "holy, holy, holy" of the seraphim expresses the superlative degree. This is not only empathetically separates God from sin but also emphasizes His righteousness in contrast to our sinfulness.

Holiness is not what God does but who He is. The Lord swears by His holiness (Amos 4:2), and He swears by Himself (Amos 6:8) they are the same. All God's attributes flow out of His holiness. That is why He is incapable of the slightest hint of impurity, unrighteousness, untruth, injustice, or questionable use of power (Gen. 18:25). Two consistent responses spring from those who have seen God's holiness: they thirst for more (Ex. 33:17-23; Ps. 42:1, 2; Phil. 3:10), and they know with certainty that He is God and they are not (Ps. 100:3).

Chapter 128
Feminism: A Social Ideology

Feminism is somewhat difficult to define, for the term means different things to different people. Some who call themselves feminists are merely interested in promoting the dignity and worth of women. Others seek to promote a specific sociopolitical ideology that goes far beyond this. Feminists raise many valid concerns: the verbal and physical abuse of women, the degradation of women through pornography, and the attitude that women are of less worth or value than men.

Feminist philosophers propose that the solution to these problems lies in women's claiming the right to name or decree meaning for themselves. They encourage women to decide who they are, what the world should be like, or who or what God is. Scripture stands against this solution. The Bible teaches that God and God alone has the right to define these things. God made the earth and created man and woman, and He has determined who they are and how they should live (Is. 45:10-13; Rom. 9:20, 21).

Women are made in the image of God (Gen. 1:27); therefore, they ought to be treated with the same dignity and respect as men. The Bible does describe, however, basic differences between men and women that are to be honored as part of God's design (1 Cor. 11:3-16). The Bible does not support the degradation or abuse of women. At the same time, it does not support the right of women (or men) to put themselves above God's plan and do as they please. Alpha woman in Christ need to respond to the real problems that feminists identify, but they must do so without compromising the plan for male and female that God has revealed in His Word.

Chapter 129
Modesty: A Measure of Propriety

Before their disobedience in the Garden, Adam and Eve "were both naked and were not ashamed" (Gen. 2:25), but afterward they were afraid. Their sense of shame and fear is at the core of modesty the need to cover out bodies. In His grace God provided clothing for the first couple, and ever since, alpha woman in Christ who fear God have covered themselves (Gen. 3:21).

The word "modesty" is quantitative in its original meaning. It has come to mean a measure of propriety or humility, characterized by reserve and freedom from excess. In the New Testament, modesty carries the idea of arrangement, not only adornment of dress but also harmony of the inner life. Its biblical meaning is a sensitive withdrawal from anything that is indelicate or impure. Throughout the Bible, lack of modesty is most often connected with an intent to commit sexual sin. Noah cursed his grandson Canaan because of the immodest actions of his father Ham (Gen. 9:21-25). Isaiah chided the women of Israel for exhibitionism (Is. 3:16). Hosea's allegory of unfaithful marriage contained reference to shameless behavior with a sexual connotation (Hos. 2:5).

Paul's writing in the New Testament refers more specifically to proper dress for believers (alpha woman in Christ). He teaches that alpha woman in Christ should know when the boundaries of decency are being overstepped. Paul assumed in teaching on spiritual gifts and proper decorum in church that certain parts of the body are to be covered (1 Cor. 12:23; 1 Tim. 2:9). The culture into which she is born and the Christian society in which she lives are factors in judging decency, but ultimately a woman's sense of modesty is to be regulated by her personal relationship with Jesus Christ and His purity.

Chapter 130
Jealousy: Adversary or Advocate?

Jealousy, unlike envy (Prov. 14:30) and covetousness, can have a positive connotation. In Scripture, the term is used to describe God's intolerance of unfaithfulness on the part of His people, especially as concerns their tendency to be drawn away by other gods (Ex. 20:5; 34:14). God's protection of His people from their enemies is the fruit of his holy jealousy (Ezek. 39:25-28). Jealousy that is the result of pride or self-centeredness is not a positive quality. It may describe the suspicions of a husband or wife in a marriage where there is unfaithfulness (Num. 5:11-31). Such human jealousy, often translated in Scripture as, "envy," easily becomes hostility toward one considered to be a rival and as such found a listing among the vices or works of the flesh (Rom. 13:13; 2 Cor. 12:20; Gal. 5:20, 21).

Such jealousy among women is not a feeling restricted to modern times. God-fearing women of old also had to deal with those feelings. Hannah longed for a child. Though she was barren, she had the devoted love of her husband Elkanah; yet the jealous and more fruitful Peninnah tormented Hannah constantly (1 Sam. 1:2-8). Peninnah's jealousy led her to treat Hannah in hurtful ways. Likewise, Rachel and Leah bickered out of jealousy (Gen. 30:15). Sarah was cruel to Hagar (Gen. 16:5, 6), jealous of her fruitfulness in bearing a son to Abraham. Instead of being advocates for one another, these women were adversaries because of their jealousies.

Luke 1:41-45 is perhaps the best example of how women might respond appropriately to one another. Elizabeth did not argue over whose child was more important. She was not envious of Mary's child; neither was Mary jealous of Elizabeth's position or marital status. Rather than snipe at each other, they encouraged and became advocates for each other. Alpha women in Christ are joint-heirs to all that belongs to Christ, which is beyond what they deserve or can even imagine (1 Cor. 2:9). They are to focus on honoring and praising God (Col. 3:1-4) and not dwell upon what they do not have or what others have, which inevitably leads to jealousy, envy, and covetousness (Ex. 20:17; 2 Cor. 10:12).

Chapter 131
Marital Conflict

Conflicts are usually the symptom of a wedge that has already been driven somehow in the past. Disagreements between spouses appear a number of times in Scripture. Solomon's poetic description of his misunderstanding with his new bride demonstrates a difference of feeling, awkward communication, and poor timing in learning to live together in love. Abraham and Sarah quarreled over her childlessness (Gen. 16:5), as did Jacob and Rachel (Gen. 30:1, 2). Job's wife disagreed with his response to his illness (Job 2:9, 10). The prophet Malachi denounced the priests who had broken, and not mended, their wedding vows (Mal. 2:14-16).

Disagreements are common, but Scripture also provides guidance. Both Paul and Peter give clues to the prevention and settlement of domestic clashes. To discordant couples in Corinth Paul wrote "God hath called us to peace" (1 Cor. 7:15). That is the ultimate objective. Peter advised wives experiencing strained relations with unbelieving husbands to win them through consistently gentle and quiet spirits (1 Pet. 3:1-4).

Human nature has not changed. Competition and contention lead only to harsh consequences. Love, on the other hand, "beareth all things, believeth all things, hopeth all things, endureth all things" (1 Cor. 13:7). Jesus taught us to remove the plank in our own eyes before we try to get rid of the specks of dust in the eyes of others (Matt. 7:3-5).

Mercy is a vital part of relaxing tensions. A patient, forgiving, tolerant spirit eases confrontations (Mic. 6:8). Sensitivity in timing also recaptures warm affection. Alpha women in Christ should not let problems fester into bitterness. The New Testament cautions us to address anger before the sun goes down (Eph. 4:26). Even if all cannot be resolved, the peace process is begun.

Finally, alpha women in Christ must choose to forgive. Calm settles over us when we allow Christ to control hurts. He modeled forgiveness (1 Pet. 2:23), and He alone can give us strength to bury revenge and to restore harmony in relationships. Alpha women in Christ are to be peacemakers (Matt. 5:9).

Chapter 132
Sexuality: A Gift from the Creator

Though the word "sex" does not occur in Scripture, the biblical language does describe God's plan for human sexual behavior, including procreation of the next generation and sexual pleasure within marriage. Sex was designed by the Creator as a special gift that allows a husband and wife to express oneness in intimate and exclusive love and to share in His plan for procreation. Sexual drives are given by God as the most natural high human bodies can experience. They are destructive only when uncontrolled or misused.

There are passages that express value for sex and celebrate it joyously (Gen. 18:12; 26:8; Song 4:1-16); others suggest abstinence from sexual activity (Ex. 19:15; 1 Sam. 21:4, 5). Deviant sexual behavior is clearly condemned: homosexuality (Lev. 18:22; Rom. 1:26, 27; 1 Cor. 6:9, 10); bestiality (Ex. 22:19; Lev. 18:23); incest (Lev. 18:6-18; 1 Cor. 5:1-13); rape (Deut. 22:23-29); prostitution (Prov. 7:1-27; 29:3). Any intimate sexual immorality (Ex. 20:14; Deut. 22:22; 1 Cor. 6:9-10). The alternative is the gift of celibacy (Matt. 19:12; 1 Cor. 7:7). Alpha women in Christ are expected to exercise self-control in overcoming improper sexual impulses, not by asceticism (Gal. 5:16-25; 1 Tim. 4:1-5) but by the power of the Holy Spirit.

Certain facts about sex should be remembered:

1. Sex is God-given (Gen. 2:18). Satan can offer nothing in the realm of sexuality except distortion and emptiness. The open discussion of sex is not wrong in itself, but it is wrong when such discussions are outside the divinely assigned context.
2. Sex between a man and a woman is different than sex in animals (Gen. 2:19, 20). Human sexuality has a specialized purpose beyond procreation.

3. Sex in the human intimacy is a total union and both powerful and mysterious (Gen. 2:21-23). God made two out of one, and the two are not complete until they are reunited. (The exception to this would be when God gives the gift of celibacy.)
4. Sex is regulated and purposeful (Gen. 2:24, 25). God Himself sets the boundary (Matt. 19:4-6). Anything short of this total and exclusive commitment between husband and wife is frustrating and destructive.

God approves the relationship in which husband and wife meet their physical needs in sexual intercourse (Prov. 5:15, 18, 19). Both husband and wife have sexual needs that are to be met in marriage (1 Cor. 7:3), and each is to meet the needs of the other and not his own.

The purpose for sexual intimacy are these:

- Knowledge (Gen. 4:1),
- Unity (Gen. 2:24),
- Comfort (Gen. 24:67),
- Procreation (Gen. 1:28),
- Relaxation and play (Song 2:8-17; 4:1-16), and
- A defense against temptation (1 Cor. 7:2-5).

A husband is commanded to find satisfaction (Prov. 5:19) and joy (Eccl. 9:9) with his wife and to concern himself with meeting her unique needs (Deut. 24:5; 1 Pet. 3:7). A wife is responsible for availability (1 Cor. 7:3-5), preparation and planning (Song 4:9), interest (Song 5:2), and sensitivity to unique masculine needs (Gen. 24:67).

Chapter 133
Romance: The Acts of Love

Scripture approved of romance unreservedly. Marriages, even when arranged, were often recorded as love matches (Gen. 24:67), and (Prov. 30:19) speaks wonderingly of the mystery of romance. Three books in Scripture, Ruth, Esther, and the Song of Solomon have romance at their center. These books are three of the five traditionally read at Jewish celebrations of the covenant between God and His people, suggesting that they have an extra dimension they do, indeed, picture the wooing of the soul by God. (Ezek. 16:4-14) recounts God's wooing of Israel; the New Testament reveals that God's love for the church is a romance that ends in marriage (2 Cor. 11:2; Rev. 21:2). Romance provides a balanced picture of God's calling of the soul: The beloved is not forced to respond but desires to respond willingly to the love offered.

Romance offers the lover an opportunity to focus on responsibilities rather than privileges. Rather than dwelling upon selfish needs what others should do, the romantic lover is ever conscious of what her or she can do to show love for the other person (Matt. 16:24-26). Everyone needs the acts of love for life and growth.

What are some basic elements of romance? Sincere admiration must be felt and shared on a regular basis (Song 1:8-10; 2:3). Differences between men and women must be acknowledged. Romance moves beyond the needs of the lover to minister to the beloved.

Chapter 134
Employment: The Challenge of a Career

The alpha woman in Christ who manages a profitable career while watching over the affairs of her household has a tremendous challenge. Frequently, her career activities take her into male-dominated arenas in which she seeks to achieve success with strength and dignity. Often her determination to seek employment is an economic necessity.

Career success does not often come easily. A woman frequently works long, hard hours and sacrifices a great deal of personal time in order to do all her jobs well. This demands unique creativity in order to maintain priorities and fulfill legitimate expectations with home and family (Eccl. 10:10). Wisdom from the Lord enables an alpha woman in Christ to prepare herself to accomplish her tasks in a way so that time and energy are used most efficiently and effectively.

By focusing on God's unconditional love a woman can keep from demanding perfection of herself. Jesus Himself finished His life on earth without healing every person who was sick or preaching to everyone who was lost (John 4:34). The challenge for alpha women in Christ with careers is to make sure that first they are women who fear the Lord and then that their work is ordered according to the priorities and plan the Lord has given.

Where does a career woman place her focus? Paul admonished women and men to seek in all pursuits to please God (1 Thess. 2:4-6). Focus on pleasing God, and He will enable you not to please others and meet their needs but also to bring honor to Him through your pursuits. In other words, He is the source of wisdom and strength to do all in a Christ-honoring way. The Lord will go with and in you to your job, and He is totally capable of helping you with any problems. He can make an enormous difference in you focus, attitude, and motivations (Col. 3:23, 24).

Chapter 135
Anger: Act or React?

Anger can most often be defined as an emotional response to a perceived wrong or injustice. Hence, anger is normally expressed when a women misinterprets circumstances, makes a mistake in judgment, or reacts quickly because she feels threatened or hurt. This anger is unjustified and sinful. This anger, in effect, denies the power of God to care for your needs and hurts and can even completely take over your life. There are many warnings about the danger of anger in Scripture (Eccl. 7:9; Matt. 5:22; Eph. 4:26, 31). Most often, alpha women in Christ should leave their anger or wrath at the feet of Jesus and allow Him to act in your behalf.

God's anger is always perfectly controlled and expressed (Ps. 30:5; 78:38). There are examples of righteous anger given in Scripture, such as Moses' anger toward the children of Israel for not trusting God and following Him (Ex. 32:19). Righteous anger can be described as one that results when God's laws and His will are knowingly disobeyed. The concern must be for righteous and reconciliation, never for personal vengeance coming out of our own hurts. We must be careful to take our anger to the Lord for Him to analyze and manage.

Do you act or react? The answer to this simple question will most likely reveal any weaknesses you have in expressing the emotion of anger. A person who acts knows who she is, what she believes and how she should behave (Col. 3:23, 24). She not only knows this information, but she chooses to act upon it. Another person's actions do not dictate her reactions, but rather the wisdom of the Lord is her mainstay (Col. 3:16, 17).

Chapter 136
Healing of Memories: A Personal Storehouse

Memories may be either conscious or unconscious; they are stored in our brains and may include thoughts, feelings, and sensory perceptions. Paul realized that he could have hidden thoughts and motives (1 Cor. 4:1-5), and David asked God to search his heart for known anxieties and any hidden wicked way (way of pain; Ps. 139:23, 24).

Memories filled with pain are frequently healed when a woman asks the Holy Spirit to touch a known memory or bring to light a hidden memory. In response this request, God sometimes allows a person to re-experience in varying degrees the hurt stored in the memory. He then enables her to choose to forgive those who victimized her and to repent of any sin of her own. As she brings her deep wound to Him for healing, He touches her and, over a period of time, takes away the pain. In its place the Lord gives her the love, acceptance, tenderness, or encouragement that she lacked from others in that situation. He does not alter the facts of the past; rather, He alters her perception of these facts. Then she is able to move forward with courage and victory in greater wholeness.

Chapter 137
The Virtuous Woman of Proverbs

Many outstanding godly women appear throughout the Bible, but the virtuous woman described here merits special praise (Prov. 31:29). This woman was a wife and mother. For centuries women have been amazed and challenged by her life (v. 31).

The passage describes what kind of wife a woman should be and what kind of woman a man should choose to marry. We were told not who she was but what she was. This woman of strength of comes alive. This rare woman was a paragon of virtue: trustworthy, industrious, organized, and loving. Yet amazingly she was able to order the priorities of her world. Her husband totally trusted her; her grown children voluntarily praised her, and her home was a model of efficiency. Still she found time to reach out to her community, to help the poor, and even to increase her family's resources through wise investments and productive management of all placed in her care. All the while, she was outwardly beautiful as she was inwardly wise.

The portrait of the virtuous woman closes with the key to her success (v. 30). Illustrating the theme of wisdom found throughout Proverbs, this woman first feared and reverenced God. Therefore, relationships and responsibilities were wisely balanced. She exemplifies the truth spoken by Jesus Christ, "Seek ye first the kingdom of God, and his righteousness; and all these things shall be added unto you" (Matt. 6:33). A close look at this woman can provide invaluable in helping every woman set her own priorities in managing the time, resources, and giftedness God has given.

Chapter 138
Covetousness: A Heart of Greed

A materialistic society demands that we constantly be in a state of acquisition for more and more. We often are mentally assaulted by messages that say, "You don't have enough, nor will you ever." "Feed with food convenient for me" (Prov. 30:8) is a refreshing cry of the heart. To realize that we can trust God to give us our portion, and that it will be sufficient, is a relief (Matt. 6:8).

When David became involved with Bathsheba, their adultery and ultimately the murder of Uriah were not his only sins. His root sin was covetousness (2 Sam. 12:1-8). God reminded David of all the people, power, and prosperity he had received. He continued, "And if that had been too little, I would moreover have given unto thee such and such things." An ungrateful heart eyes that continue to seek more can lead to deadly consequences.

To free your heart of covetousness:

- Repent of a discontented heart (Phil. 4:11, 12).
- Set your heart on things eternal (1 John 2:15-17).
- Trust that God will keep His promises (Phil. 4:19; Heb. 13:5).
- Yield to God's plan for your life (2 Cor. 9:8-10).

Chapter 139
Favoritism: The Need for Equal Love

Though a parent may feel a special rapport with a child same interests, similar physical characteristics, compatible goals a parent err in consistently offering special consideration, responsibility, or privilege to one child to the exclusion of another (Gen. 25:28). Some parents favor beauty or intellect; others elevate the child who is difficult or a troublemaker. Some seek to undercut the brighter child or more spiritually sensitive child in order to compensate for her sibling who is not gifted in the same way.

One child may be showered with attention and the others ignored (Gen. 37:3). Anger, resentment, and insecurity will arise in the child denied (v. 4); guilt and defensiveness or even tyranny may characterize the one singled out for attention (vv. 5-11). A child may also be singled out for criticism and unrealistic expectations with the burden of never being able to measure up (Prov. 11:29).

Each child should be given praise and recognition in inclusive, not exclusive, ways (Prov. 25:11). A parent should build on a child's strengths, allowing for differences (Prov. 24:3). A child should be enjoyed and accepted for who she is, not what she may do for you. Comparison must be avoided (2 Cor. 10:12). A parent does well to love equally but appreciate individually (Ps. 32:8). Fair and equal are not synonymous, but both are necessary in relating to children.

Chapter 140
Gossip: Controlling Your Tongue

Most of us are not strangers to gossip, we have listened to it, spread it, and been the victim of it. Rumors have a dangerous edge in that people do not feel responsible for that which they simply pass on as hearsay, making accountability and damage control much more difficult. Gossip can run the gamut from talk of a personal, sensational, or intimate nature to statements that defame or injure the reputation or wellbeing of a person. Often our conversations are full of judgments. The Lord lists gossips together with the untrustworthy, unloving, unrighteous, murderers, and haters of God. (Rom. 1:28-32). The Bible is clear about the damage (Prov. 11:13; 16:28; 18:6-8; 26:20) and consequences of gossip and slander (Ps. 101:5; Prov. 8:13; 17:9; Matt. 12:36, 37; 1 Tim. 5:13).

Not only the spreading of lies but also the telling of partially or entirely true facts may yet fall under the wrath of God. Sharing anything about a person that does not help or edify may be considered gossip. God has his own plan for dealing with someone in sin (Matt. 18:15). We are to go to an offending individual and no one else to begin a longsuffering effort for their restoration to God id we are concerned about their eternal welfare (Gal. 6:1). Listening to gossip is just as bad as spreading the words of hurt (1 Sam. 24:9; Prov. 17:4). A mark of spiritual maturity is to have control over your tongue (James 1:26). Gossip and slander are tools of Satin.

In Paul's discussion of the holy lifestyle in which spiritually mature women are to teach younger women, he includes a warning about slander and admonishes the women not to accuse others ("the accuser," a title assigned to Satan 34 times in Scripture), thus refraining from being "devils" in their relationships. Nothing is a sharper sword with which to wound another than hurtful words. Gossip is never an act of kindness: it diminishes the person about whom you are talking; it degrades any Christian who would do such thing; it serves as a temptation and snare to any listener who would join in such unkindness.

Chapter 141

Homemaking: An Expression of Creativity and Love

King Solomon identified three great foundation stones of a home:

1. Wisdom knowledge of God's ways and the ability to make right choices in both practical and ethical matters.
2. Understanding an ability to apply God's principles, especially to relationships, and
3. Knowledge very practical skills in specific areas (Prov. 24:3, 4).

The home is the primary place where children and parents learn God's wisdom and how to apply it to their lives, where loving relationships are built on mutual communication and understanding, and where children and adults both learn and grown in the basic practical skills needed for life to function smoothly.

A woman's role involves role involved helping family members get along with one another in the context of the home and creating an environment in which each family member might feel fully at ease, nurtured, and safe. Home is expected to be a place of refuge from life's storms. A woman's homemaking ability should be infused with creativity and love so that her home reflects her own personal style. Homemaking skills were highly prized in Bible times, and the training of young women focused primarily on the care of husbands, children, and home (Titus 2:3-5).

Homemaking from a biblical perspective, however, is not limited to the care of physical property or the meeting of physical needs but extends to the creation of a nurturing and satisfying environment in which a family might flourish emotionally and spiritually. In the context of such a home our identities are forged in a healthy and positive way, and we truly become equipped to minister to others. A home built on the Lord Jesus and nurtured by a woman who spends time seeking wisdom, understanding, and knowledge with the Lord Jesus each day will stand strong in the storms of life.

Chapter 142
Substance Abuse: The Devastation of Drugs

Drugs are used by many as a way to avoid emotional pain. The pain of past or present hurts, or future fears. The impact of drugs on the individual, her family, and others is devastating. Family and friends, however, often find themselves unwittingly aiding the abuser in her denial process by making excuses or refusing to accept that she is harming herself and them. As long as she is able to deny her behavior, she will not see the need for change.

Although alcohol is the drug to which most frequent reference is made in the Bible and also the one more often used by people today, Scripture refers to two other situations where drugs may well have been involved: witchcraft or sorcery, and idolatry. Grim warning is given to those who practice those activities (Gal. 5:19-21). God encourages us as alpha women in Christ to bring our cares to Him (Ps. 55:22; 1 Pet. 5:6, 7) instead of trying to handle them alone or escape from them by using chemicals or any other artificial means. He stands willing to forgive those who have been involved with drugs or any other harmful substance if we ask for His forgiveness (1 John 1:9).

Alpha women in Christ are exhorted to be filled with and to walk by the Spirit instead of being dependent upon wine (Gal. 5:16, 25; Eph. 5:18). What is said about wine applies to the use of any chemical that alters behavior and has the potential to become addictive. Facing the problem of substance abuse and giving it over to God, confident that He is able to deliver you and bring you through the pain and out of the bondage, puts a person on the road to recovery and victory (Rom. 4:20, 21).

Chapter 143
Gluttony: An Undisciplined Appetite

Scripture speaks especially harshly about gluttony linking it with poverty. Gluttony can indicate excessive eating and drinking, and it does refer to a ravenous, nearly unstoppable, appetite. It is to food what greed is to material wealth, a craving that cannot be satisfied. More specifically, in Scripture gluttony is associated with eating foods forbidden to the Israelites, the meat and delicacies that are called "deceptive meals" (Prov. 23:1-3, 20, 21). It was also associated with a loose and undisciplined lifestyle disobedience, stubbornness, and rebellion (Deut. 21:20). The fruits of gluttony were laziness and poverty to the glutton (Prov. 23:21) and shame to others (Prov. 28:7).

Gluttony has been smiled upon in modern times. Though never listed on the death certificate, you would probably be amazed at how many diseases have gluttony as a root cause. Solomon prescribed drastic measures if a person is "given to appetite." He said, "Put a knife to thy throat" (Prov. 23:2), a stern and severe way of dealing with an undesirable habit or a health problem.

Daniel recognized that food and drink affected nutrition and health (Dan. 1:8, 12-16), and Solomon speaks of deceitful "dainties," or delicacies, and warns us not to desire them (Prov. 23:3). Many modern foods have been robbed of their vital nutrients and contain ingredients that may fill our bodies with elements that take the place of nutritious foods. The gluttonous use of foods high in sugar and fat takes away from the nutritional balance of milk, fruit, vegetables, meat and bread, which contain fiber and other nutrients for good digestion and health. First and foremost, we are not to satisfy our selfish and harmful appetites but rather use our bodies to bring glory to God (1 Cor. 6:19, 20).

Chapter 144
Children: Discipline from Parents

Parenthood involves a process of making disciples of your own children. Parents teach obedience not just to bring children under parental authority but in order to bring them to salvation and spiritual discipleship (Heb. 12:11). While punishment may sometimes be a part of discipline, much more is involved in moving a child from parent-controlled behavior to self-controlled, independent decision making and ultimately to a God-controlled lifestyle in which the child learns to make wise, God-honoring decisions on his own (Heb. 12:10-11). Godly discipline provides an umbrella of protection under which a child learns to obey God during the days of vulnerability.

Willful defiance is a deliberate act of disobedience in which a child knows what his parents expect, then chooses to do the opposite (Prov. 29:1). This is to be distinguished from childish irresponsibility, resulting from forgetting, making mistakes, having a short attention span or low frustration tolerance, or immaturity. To nurture and control children demands enough firmness to correct unacceptable behavior (Prov. 22:15) but not so much as to injure or damage a child (Eph. 6:4). Loving parents, who exhibit a tenderness, kindness, and gentleness no matter what the child's behavior, err when they intervene to protect the child from reaping the consequences of that behavior (Prov. 13:24).

Guidelines are given for administering the rod of discipline, which, as a symbol of the parent's loving care and concern, should be administered only in love. The rod underscores the responsibility of the individual for his own attitudes, actions, and reactions (Ezek. 18:20; Rom. 3:23; 14:12). Correction shows the child the error of his way and pulls him to the right way. Discipline should be delivered promptly at the time of the offense (Prov. 13:24), catching . wrong behavior patterns before they become set. The child must understand clearly that the behavior was wrong (Col. 3:25) and that the authority violated is not merely that of the earthly parent, but of God. The child must be led to evaluate his action as sin, and he must be led to see the need of seeking forgiveness and changing direction. The child should see grief reflected in the parent (Prov. 17:25), who should remain with the child until their fellowship has been restored (Ps. 51:7-12). In this light, Proverbs 22:6 is not just a promise to good parents that consistent spiritual nurture ultimately assures their children of godly lives, but it also a warning that leaving a child to the willfulness of going his own way is the path to destruction (Prov. 3:5, 6), laying a foundation for self-willed living from which the child will not depart (Judg. 21:25; Prov. 3:5; 12:15; 14:12; 21:2; 29:15; Is. 53:6).

Chapter 145

PMS (Premenstrual Syndrome): Coping with Your Body Cycle

PMS (premenstrual syndrome) includes a wide variety of physical and psychological symptoms that may recur during the menstrual cycle. Traits such as being argumentative, combative, angry, and vexing (Prov. 21:19) are commonplace among women suffering from PMS. Medical studies reveal that only 10 percent of the menstruating-aged female population are completely free of PMS symptoms; the other 90 percent struggle to some degree.

Would it really be better to live alone, hungry and thirsty in a desert rather than to live with a woman who exhibits these characteristics? Some husbands think so (Prov. 12:4; 19:13; 21:9, 19; 25:24; 27:15). If you suffer from the extreme symptoms of PMS, realize that it is a physical illness and should be given serious medical attention. Severe PMS can even lead to alarming problems such as child abuse, marital conflict, divorce, depression, and suicide. Seek out a physician who can help you take care of your body, which is the temple of the Lord (2 Cor. 6:16).

Chapter 146
Humor: A Time to Laugh

The psalmist declares that God Himself sits in the heavens and laughs (Ps. 2:4), and the writer of Proverbs describes the woman of strength as one who rejoices in times to come (Prov. 31:25). Life can becoming taxing at times, and moments come when we desperately need a change. Laughter is one way the Creator gave us to switch gears and punctuate monotony with joy. Humor is an exit from the mundane road of life. Laughter is a simple yet reasonable prescription for life's ills and most of its tedium (Prov. 17:22). Physicians have assigned healing properties to humor, especially in cases of mental illness, such as depression. Certainly humor defuses tensions and helps put at ease.

With so much tragedy in life, choosing humor instead of despair is good scriptural advice. Humor generally involves an acceptance of ups and downs of life and the determination not to take ourselves too seriously. To combat stress, to relieve tension, and even to provide, delightful diversion in the midst to trials and sufferings, laughter and a keen sense of humor may prove to be precious possessions.

Jesus Himself was unpredictable and witty and full of life in His responses. He used irony, word play, and hyperbole to get across His messages (Matt. 22:15-22), in which Jesus cleverly eludes the trap of the Pharisees and unmasks their hypocrisy. Jesus asks a Pharisee for a coin with an image of Caesar and an inscription proclaiming Caesar to be god, knowing that to carry such a coin was breaking two commandments (Ex. 20:3, 4). At the end of life's road we may all end up in the same place someday, but because of laughter along the way, some will have enjoyed the journey and arrived more refreshed.

Chapter 147
Inheritance: Passing It On

Every home should provide a storehouse of happy memories. God knows us even before we are formed. Aunts, uncles, grandparents, and parents should be challenged to link hand and heart to provide a vital, living example of what true Christianity is all about (Ps. 78:4-6). God's plan is for godly heritage to begin before birth. The privilege and blessings of the extended family provide untold blessings. The influence of grandparents in forming values and character cannot be underestimated. The valuable advice of parents, the care and concern of brothers and sisters, the influence of all family members on the children is vitally important to the development of godly character in a child.

The unique privileges and tremendous responsibility of providing influence and atmosphere are not confined to the walls of the parental home. The potential influence of a faithful grandparent and God-fearing parent is unending. Principles and precepts are shared in the family's faith journey from generation to generation by parents, grandparents, and great-grandparents. The godly men and women who make up our spiritual heritage (Deut. 5:29) and who consider the passing on of the instructions given to Moses a priority (Deut. 6:6, 7). Such a spiritual inheritance will outlive its own generation, brining strength and joy to our children's children as they experience ups and downs, difficulties, problems, and, of course, the faithfulness of God.

Deuteronomy 6 directs parents to pass along their spiritual heritage throughout the course of any given day when working in the kitchen, carpooling to school, sitting around the breakfast table, or watching TV in the evenings. There are no set times or specific locations to pass on our values and spiritual legacy. This passage implies a lifestyle modeling and discussion of those things that are deeply important to us. If these values are not woven through the everyday cloth of normal life, then the fabric of life is weak indeed.

Our task is not to showcase perfect families within our communities but rather to allow an unbelievable world to see ordinary families struggling with real issues, yet finding strength and wisdom in a loving, sufficient Savior.

Chapter 148
Parenthood: A God-Given Responsibility

Something must be incredibly basic, important, and possible in parenthood if being parents is part of the primary command God gave to the mother and father of the human race (Gen. 1:28). True, reproduction was necessary to continue the generations, but to see children as simply the byproduct of a biological function is to miss completely the divine significance attached to parenthood (Ps. 127; 128).

God made us in His image (Gen. 1:27), and nothing reveals the true nature of His deity any more than God's loving creation of human life. How could man and woman more unambiguously reflect that characteristic of God than in their own loving procreation of a child?

The Bible contains clear principles for rearing children in the nurture and admonition of the Lord.

- Parents are to demonstrate God's pattern for Christian marriage (1 Tim. 3:4, 12; Titus 2:1-5). A loving relationship between mother and father is a living object lesson for the child in how a husband and wife are to relate in marriage.
- Parents are responsible for teaching their children spiritual truths (Deut. 6:4-9; Ps. 78:1-8; 2 Tim. 1:3-5; Eph. 6:4). Such an important task cannot be left to the church and Christian school.
- Parents must lead their children to go God's way through loving and consistent discipline (Prov. 13:24; 19:18; 20:30; 22:15; Heb. 12:5-8, 11). This is not merely administering punishment but careful nurture to make disciples out of their children, teaching them how to live the Christian life by word and example.

Chapter 149
Wisdom: Its Foundation and Expression

Fear of the Lord is the foundation for wisdom, the prerequisite for obedience, and the accompaniment of love (Deut. 10:12). Fearing the Lord and loving Him are not antithetical but inseparable responses. The Book of Proverbs is permeated with these admonitions (Prov. 1:7; 31:30). Other wisdom literature supports the plea (Eccl. 12:13), the prophets echo the same (Mic. 6:8), and the New Testament picks up this emphasis in its description of "a gentle and quiet spirit" (1 Pet. 3:4).

"Fear" in this sense indicates submissive reverence and not stark terror. To reject this awe, which inspires respectful obedience, is to determine to go your own way (Prov. 1:31) and turn away from God's way (Is. 55:8). The promised results of fearing Him are goodness, riches, honor, and satisfaction (Ps. 31:19), a right relationship with others (Lev. 25:17), long life (Deut. 6:2), mercy (Ps. 103:17), strong confidence (Prov. 14:26), and God's constant attention (Ps. 34:7).

Chapter 150
Girlhood: The Bud of Womanhood

A surface reading of the Bible may leave a young girl with the impression that this Book is of little relevance to her today. Only a few times are young girls specifically mentioned in the history of God's dealings with His people.

Rebekah in her youth was beautiful and charming as well as gracious and resourceful. She became the wife of the patriarch Isaac (Gen. 24:15-67). Naaman's young maidservant was not only obedient and helpful but also spiritually perceptive as she was responsible for introducing her pagan master to the God of Israel (2 Kin. 5:1-14). The daughter of Jairus was a member of a prominent and wealthy household, but she was also valuable to the Savior who restored her to life (Mark 5:21-43). The girl Rhoda was alert and sensitive to the working of the Lord in delivering Peter from prison, and she refused to doubt even when others questioned her faith (Acts 12:13-15).

In addition, to these examples is the vibrant testimony of Mary, the mother of our Lord. In her youth probably her teens she showed remarkable faith and commitment as she responded with obedience to God's call to her (Luke 1:26-38). Scripture clearly affirms the relevance and sufficiency of the Bible for all Christians of all times (1 Tim. 3:16; 2Pet. 1:3) because the most fundamental issues of human life resurface in every generation.

Proverbs, the only book specifically addressed to young people, is essentially a book about pure living and wise decision making. Its advice for boys is equally appropriate for girls. The Book of Numbers is primarily the story of the Israelites in the wilderness in their time between leaving Mount Sinai and entering the Promise Land, but a close study of it can offer girls insights into the trials that they are likely to face as they mature from girlhood to womanhood. Girlhood is a time of identity formation, self-discovery, friendship, and growth, and God's Word is sufficient to guide girls in all these areas.

Chapter 151
Femininity: The Nature of Woman

Femininity is a reality of God's design and making His precious gift to every woman and, in a very different way, His gracious gift to men as well. The difference between men and women is not a mere matter of biology. Throughout the millennia of human history, up until the past several decades, people took for granted that the differences were so obvious as to need no comment. Yet never as now have we more needed Paul's reminder to the Roman Christians not to let the world squeeze us into its own mold but to let God remold our minds from within (Rom. 12:2).

Surrender is a key ingredient in femininity. As a bride, a woman in marriage surrenders her independence, her name, her destiny, her will, and ultimately, in the marriage chamber, her body, to the bridegroom. As a mother, she surrenders in a very real sense her life of the child. As a single woman, she surrenders herself in a unique way for service to her Lord and for service to family and community.

Femininity receives. It takes what God gives. In other words, women are to receive the given as Mary did (Luke 1:38), not to insist upon the not-given, as Eve did (Gen. 3:1-6). This does not imply that a woman should surrender to evils such as coercion or violent conquest. The gentle and quiet spirit of which Peter speaks is the ornament of femininity (1 Pet. 3:4), which found its epitome in Mary, the mother of Jesus. She was willing to be a vessel, hidden, unknown, except as Somebody's mother. This maternity is available to every alpha woman in Christ who humbles herself before the Lord, not simply as a biological role but as an attitude of selflessness in her own heart and submission to the Lord.

The challenge of biblical femininity for you is to be a woman, holy through and through asking for nothing but what God wants to give you, receiving with both hands and with all your heart whatever that is. Femininity is a precious treasure to be guarded and nourished each and every day.

References

Pauline Albenda, "Westen Asiatic Women in the Iron Age: Their Image Revealed," Biblical Archaeologist 46 (Spring 1983).

"Albright the Beautician Reveals Secret of Queen Esther's Cosmetic Aid," Biblical Archaeology Review 2 (March 1976).

Betsy Halpern Amaru, "Portraits of Biblical Women in Josephus' Antiquities," Journal of Jewish Studies 39 (Autumn 1988). Ruth Amiram, Ancient Pottery of the Holy Land (Jerusalem: Masada Press, 1969).

Nachman Avigad, "How the Wealthy Lived in Herodian Jerusalem," Biblical Archaeology Review 2 (December 1976).

Nahaman Avigad, "Jerusalem in Flames-The Burnt House Captures a Moment in Time," Biblical Archaeology Review 9 (November/December 1983).

Clinton Bailey, "How Desert Culture Helps Us Understand the Bible: Bedouin Law Explains Reaction to Rape of Dinah," Bible Review 7 (August 1991).

Gabriel Barkay, "The Divine Name Found in Jerusalem," Bible Review 7 (March/April 1983).

Bathja Bayer, "The Finds That Could Not Be," Biblical Archaoelogy Review 8 (January/February 1982).

E.M. Blaiklock, "A Chronological Table of Archaeologists and Their Work," Zandervan Pictorial Encyclopedia of the Bible (Grand Rapids, Michigan: Zondervan, 1975) vol. 1, pp. 266-277.

E.M. Blaiklock and R.K Harrison, eds., The New International Dictionary of Biblical Archaeology (Grand Rapids, Michigan: Zondervan 1983).

George J. Brooke, "Power to the Powerless – A Long-Last Song of Miriam," Biblical Archaeology Review 20 (May/June 1994).

Magen Broshi, "Beware the Wiles of the Wanton Woman," Biblical Archaeology Review 9 (July/August 1983).

Trent C. Butler, ed., The Holman Bible Dictionary (Nashville Tennessee: Holman Bible Publishers, 1991).

"Buzz or Button," Biblical Archaeology Review 17 (May/June 1991).

Jane Cahill, Karl Reinhard, David Tarler, and Peter Warnock, "Scientists Examine Remains of Ancient Bathroom," Biblical Archaeology Review 17 (May/June 1991).

"Glossary: How to Date a Cooking Pot," Biblical Archaeology Review 18 (September/ 1992).

"Is the Cultic Installation at Dan Really an Olive Press?" Biblical Archaeology Review 10 (November/December 1984).

Kathleen Kenyon, Digging Up Jericho (1957), Excavations at Jericho, 2 vols. (1960, 1965),

Archaeology in the Holy Land (1960), The Bible and Recent Archaeology (1978).

Ann Killebrew and Steven Fine, "Qatzrin: Reconstructing Village Life in Talmudic Times," Biblical Archaeology Review 17 (May/June 1991).

Barbara S. Lesko, "Women's Monumental Mark on Ancient Egypt," Biblical Archaeology 54 (March 1991): 4-15

Herbert Lockyer, Sr., ed., Nelson's Illustrated Bible Dictionary (Nashville Tennessee: Thomas Nelson Publisher, 1986).

Carol L. Meyers, "Of Drums and Damsels," Biblical Archaeologist 54 (March 1991).

Peter Roger Stuart Moorey, "British Women in Near Eastern Archaeology: Kathleen Kenyon and the Pioneers," Palestine Exploration Quarterly 124 (July-December 1992).

Kjeld Nielsen, "Ancient Aromas Good and Bad," Bible Review 7 (June 1991).

"The Patriarchs' Wives as Sisters-Is the Anchor Bible Wrong?" Biblical Archaeology Review 1 (September 1975).

Shalom M. Paul, "Jerusalem of Gold-A Song and an Ancient Crown," Biblical Archaeology Review 3 (December 1977).

Charles R. Pfeiffer, ed., The Biblical World: A Dictionary of Biblical Archaeology (Grand Rapids, Michigan: Baker Book House, 1966).

John B. Polhill, Acts, The New American Commentary, vol. 26 (Nashville Tennessee: Broadman Press, 1992), p. 349, footnote 24.

H. Rand, "Figure-Vases in Ancient Egypt and Hebrew Midwives," Israel Exploration Quarterly 20:3-4 (1970).

Stan Rummel, "Clothes Maketh the Man – An Insight from Ancient Ugarit," Biblical Archaeology Review 2 (June 1976).

Marla J. Selvidge, "Mark 5:25-34 and Leviticus 15:19-20: A Reaction to Restrictive Purity Regulations," Journal of Biblical Literature 103 (December 1984).

Neil Asher Silberman, "Restoring the Reputation of Lady Hester Lucy Stanhope: A Little-known Episode in the Beginnings of Archaeology in the Holy Land," Biblical Archaeology Review 10 (July/August 1984).

Brunilde Sismondo Ridgway, "Ancient Greek Women and Art: The Material Evidence," American Journal of Archaeology 91 (July 1987).

Michael T. Shoemaker, "Herod's Lady's Earring?" Biblical Archaeology Review 17 (July/August 1991).

Lawrence E. Stager, "Eroticism & Infanticide at Ashkelon," Biblical Archaeology Review 17 (July/August 1991).

William H. Stephens, The New Testament World in Pictures (Nashville, Tennessee: Broadman Press, 1987).

Robert R. Stieglitz, "The Minoan Origin of Tyrian Purple," Biblical Archaeologist 54 (March 1994).

Varda Sussman, "Lighting the Way Through History: The Evolution of Ancient Oil Lamps," Biblical Archaeology Review 11 (March/April 1985).

Danny Syon, "Gamla-Portrait of a Rebellion," Biblical Archaeology Review 18 (January/February 1992).

Merrill C. Tenney, The Zondervan Pictorial Encyclopedia of the Bible, 5 vols. (Grand Rapids, Michigan: Zondervan, 1975).

Paula Wapnish, "Beauty and Utility in Bone-New Light on Bone Crafting," Biblical Archaeology Review 17 (July/August 1991).

Elizabeth Lyding Will, "Women in Pompeii," Archaeology 32 (September/October 1979).

"You Can Never Find One When You Need One," Biblical Archaeology Review 18 (November/December 1992).

Sybil Zimmerman, "Housewares and Recipes from 2000 Years Ago," Biblical Archaeology Review 7 (September/October 1981).

Selected Sources for Inspirational Quotations

Catherine Booth. Aggressive Christianity copyright by Worldwide Publications.

Jill Briscoe. De-Baiting the Woman Trap copyright 1994 by Jill Briscoe. Published by Baker Books. Used by permission.

Nancie Carmichael. Virtue March/April 1995. Used by permission.

Rhonda De Sola Chervin, comp. Quotable Saints copyright 1992 by Rhonda De Sola Chervin, published by Servant Publications.

Mary C. Crowley. Think Mink! Copyright 1976 by Fleming H. Revell Company.

Linda Dillow. Creative Counterpart copyright 1977, 1986 by Linda Dillow. Published by Thomas Nelson, Inc.

Cindy Lewis Dake. Contempo May 1992. Published by the Women's Missionary Union, Southern Baptist Convention.

Elisabeth Elliot. Let Me Be a Woman copyright 1976 by Tyndale House Publishers, Inc. A Slow and Certain Light copyright 1973 by Elisabeth Elliot Leitch. Published by Word, Inc. A Path Through Suffering copyright 1990 by Elisabeth Elliot Gren. Published by Servant Publications.

Mary Farrar. Christian Book Review May/June 1995.

Joy P. Gage. Every Woman's Privilege copyright 1986 by Joy Gage, published by Multnomah Press. Also, Mrs. Gage as quoted in Heart to Heart with Pastor's Wives, compiled by Lynne Dugan. Copyright 1994 by Lynne Dugan. Published by Regal Books, a division of Gospel Light.

Gloria Gaither, Gigi Graham Tchividjian, Susan Alexander Yates. Marriage: Questions Women Ask copyright 1992 by Christianity Today, Inc. Published by Multnomah Press.

Ruth Bell Graham. Quoted in Today's Christian Woman January/February 1991.

Catherine Hickem. Quoted in Heart to Heart with Pastor's Wives, compiled by Lynne Dugan.

Copyright 1994 by Lynne Dugan. Published by Regal Books, a division of Gospel Light.

Susan Hunt. Spiritual Mothering copyright 1992 by Susan Hunt. Published by Legacy Communications.

Helen Keller. Quoted in Great Quotes from Great Women copyright 1991 by Celebrating Excellence, Inc.

Rhonda Harrington Kelley. Divine Discipline copyright 1992 by Rhonda Harrignton Kelley, published by Pelican Publishing Company, Inc.

Carol Kent. Today's Christian Woman. Interview by Jan L. Senn. 1995.

Beverly LaHaye. The Spirit-Controlled Woman copyright 1976 by Harvest House Publishers

Jo Ann Paris Leavell. Joy in the Journey copyright 1994 by Jo Ann Paris Leavell, published by Pelican Publishing Company, Inc.

Gail MacDonald. Quoted in Heart to Heart with Pastor's Wives, compiled by Lynne Dugan.

Copyright 1994 by Lynne Dugan. Published by Regal Books, a division of Gospel Light.

Karen Mains. Open Heart, Open Home copyright 1976 by David C. Cook Publishers. Making Sunday Special copyright 1984 by Karen Mains. Published by Word Books.

Mary Ann Mayo. Virtue May/June 1995.

Henrietta Mears. What the Bible Is All About copyright 1953, 1954, 1960, 1966 by Gospel Light Publications. Revised edition copyright 1983. Published by Regal Books.

Mother Teresa of Calcutta. Quoted in Journey Magazine November 1994. Published by the Baptist Sunday School Board.

Anne Ortlund. Disciplines of the Beautiful Woman copyright 1977, 1984 by Word, Inc. Disciplines of the Heart copyright by Word, Inc. Dorothy Kellley Patterson. A Woman Seeking God (Nashville: Broadman Press, 1988). All rights reserved.

Amy Roth. Quoted in Journey Magazine November 1994. Published by the Baptist Sunday School Board.

Jan Silvious. Meditations for the Busy Woman copyright 1993 by Jan Silvious.

Jeanette Thomason. Virtue March/April 1995.

Lila Trotman. Quoted in The Spirit-Controlled Woman by Beverly LaHaye. Copyright 1976 by Harvest House Publishers.

Bertha Von Suttner. Quoted in Great Quotes from Great Women copyright 1991 by Celebrating Excellence, Inc.

Mary Welchel. The Christian Working Woman copyright 1989, 1994. Published by Revell.

Sheila West. Quoted in Journey Magazine, published 1995 by the Baptist Sunday School Board.

Heather Whitestone. Christian Single January 1995. Interview by Amy Adams. Published by the Baptist Sunday School Board.

Mary Lou Whitlock. Quoted in Heart to Heart with Pastor's Wives, compiled by Lynne Dugan.

Copyright 1994 by Lynne Dugan Published by Regal Books, a division of Gospel Light.

"Getting to Know the Author" by Anne Graham Lotz, excerpted from God's Story (Nashville, TN: W Publishing Group, 1999), pp. viii-xl (prologue) copyright 1999 by AGL.

"A Balanced Spiritual Diet" by Nany Leigh DeMoss, excerpted from A Place of Quiet Rest (Chicago: Moody Publishers, 2000), pp. 168-172, copyright 2000 by Nancy Leigh DeMoss.

"Beginning to Read and Study the Bible" by Roberta Hromas, excerpted from Passport to the Bible (Wheaton, IL: Tyndale House, 1980), copyright by Roberta Hromas.

"The Word of God: A Precious Treasure" by Nancy Leigh DeMoss, excerpted from A Place of Quiet Rest, pp. 146-149.

"A Deeper Walk of Faith" by Emilie Barnes, adapted from More Faith in My Day (Eugene, OR: Harvest House Publishers, 2005), pp. 7-8, copyright 2005 by Bob and Emilie Barnes; and from 15 Minutes Alone with God (Eugene, OR: Harvest House Publishers House.

"Jesus, God's Refreshing Word," by Dee Brestin and Kathy Troccoli, excerpted from Forever in Love with Jesus (Nashville, TN: W Publishing Group 2004), pp. 65-68, copyright 2004 by Dee Brestin and Kathy Troccoli.

"Walking in the Light of the Word," by Kimberly Daniels, adapted from Clean House Strong